Trade, Gender,

Intersectional Approaches to Sustainable Development

Commonwealth Secretariat

The Commonwealth

Commonwealth Secretariat
Marlborough House
Pall Mall
London SW1Y 5HX
United Kingdom

© Commonwealth Secretariat 2020

All rights reserved. No part of this publication may be reproduced, stored in a retrieval system, or transmitted in any form or by any means, electronic or mechanical, including photocopying, recording or otherwise without the permission of the publisher.

Published by the Commonwealth Secretariat

Typeset by Nova Techset, Chennai, India
Printed by APS Group

Views and opinions expressed in this publication are the responsibility of the author(s) and should in no way be attributed to the institutions to which they are affiliated or to the Commonwealth Secretariat.

The original conceptualisation and scoping for this research project was by Olayinka Bandele.

Wherever possible, the Commonwealth Secretariat uses paper sourced from responsible forests or from sources that minimise a destructive impact on the environment.

Copies of this publication may be obtained from:

Publications Section
Commonwealth Secretariat
Marlborough House
Pall Mall
London SW1Y 5HX
United Kingdom
Tel: +44 (0)20 7747 6534
Email: publications@commonwealth.int
Web: https://books.thecommonwealth.org/

A catalogue record for this publication is available from the British Library.

ISBN (paperback): 978-1-84929-195-8
ISBN (e-book): 978-1-84859-987-1

About the Authors

Mariama Williams, Ph.D. is Coordinator for Sustainable Development, Climate Change and Gender (SDCCG) at the South Centre, an inter-governmental think tank of developing countries. She is a feminist economist with over 30 years' experience of working on economic development, macroeconomics and trade and finance issues. She focuses on gender equality, women's empowerment and social equity, external debt and finance and, more recently, climate change. She is also a director of the Institute of Law and Economics (ILE) in Jamaica. Her current areas of research are South-South Cooperation (with a focus on climate change finance), climate change adaptation, gender and climate change, the economics of climate change, macroeconomics and sustainable development in the context of the implementation of the 2030 Agenda. Her publications include *Gender and Climate Financing: Coming Out of the Margin* (Routledge, 2015), 'Africa and the World Trade Organization' in *Africa and the World: Global Politics, Diplomacy, and International Relations* (Nagar et. al., I.B Tauris, 2017), 'Promoting Sustainable Development by Addressing the Impacts of Climate Change Response Measures on Developing Countries' (with Martin Khor et al., South Centre, 2017), *Trading Stories: Experiences with Gender and Trade* (with Marilyn Carr, Commonwealth Secretariat, 2009) and *Gender Issues in the Multilateral Trading System: A Reference Manual* (Commonwealth Secretariat, 2003). She is also a lead author for Chapter 15, Investment and Finance, Working Group III (Mitigation), the Sixth Assessment Report (AR6) of the Inter-Governmental Panel on Climate Change (IPCC).

Olayinka Bandele, BA (Hon) Econ, MSc (Econ), MSc (Business) is a Trade Adviser in the Trade, Oceans and Natural Resources Directorate at the Commonwealth Secretariat. She is a development economist with 20 years' experience of working on trade policy, private sector development, export strategy, export diversification, SME trade and the intersectionality of trade and gender. She is currently focusing on the design and implementation of trade programmes to support developing countries' trade policy development objectives. She was previously an Overseas Development Institute (ODI) fellow and senior economist/manager of Private Sector Development at Nathan EME Inc. She regularly acts as a discussant or peer reviewer for research by other trade development agencies; most recently, she participated in the UNCTAD Women in Cross Border Trade in East Africa conference in Tanzania in November 2019. She is the series editor of the *Commonwealth Trade Competitiveness Briefing Paper* series and the *Commonwealth Trade Express* series. Her publications include 'An Equal Seat at the Table: Gendering Trade Policy' (*International Trade Working Paper*, Commonwealth Secretariat, 2016), which was originally a background paper to the *Commonwealth Trade Review 2015*, the Secretariat's flagship trade publication.

Acknowledgements

Mariama Williams, lead author, is thankful to Peter Lunenborg (Trade for Development Programme, South Centre) for his light touch review of particular trade elements of the publication. Thanks is also extended to Val Mims who provided editorial service for the publication during its many iterations.

Olayinka Bandele would like to acknowledge and thank peer reviewer Jennifer Namgyal (Gender Adviser, Gender Unit, Commonwealth Secretariat) for her insightful observations on the penultimate version of the manuscript. Appreciation is also extended to blind peer reviewer Lebohang Liepollo Pheko (Senior Research Fellow, Trade Collective Member) for undertaking the challenge to critically review the manuscript.

The views expressed in this publication are those of the authors and do not necessarily reflect the official position or policy of the Commonwealth Secretariat, the South Centre or any other agency or government identified.

Contents

About the Authors	iii
Acknowledgements	v
Abbreviations and Acronyms	ix
Summary	xiii

1 Introduction — 1
Notes — 6

2 The Nexus of Gender, Trade, Climate and Sustainable Development — 9
2.1 Gender and sustainable development — 11
2.2 Trade and sustainable development — 12
2.3 Gender and trade — 13
2.4 Climate change and sustainable development — 17
2.5 Gender and climate change — 23
2.6 Interlinkages between trade and climate at sectoral levels – implications for gender equality and women's economic empowerment — 26
Notes — 47

3 Gender Issues in Trade and Climate Change Governance — 53
3.1 Gender and governance issues within the trade debate — 53
3.2 Gender issues in climate governance — 65
3.3 Gender and climate policy in Commonwealth developing countries — 68
Notes — 70

4 Exploring the Linkages Between the Governance of Climate Change and the Governance of International Trade — 75
4.1 Trade issues in the climate governance framework — 76
4.2 Climate issues and trade governance — 77
4.3 Linkages between climate change and trade – relevance for inclusive sustainable growth and women's empowerment — 80
4.4 Gendering the trade–climate policy nexus — 83
Notes — 86

5 Summary, Recommendations and Way Forward — 89
5.1 Summary — 89
5.2 Recommendations and way forward — 90
Notes — 97

Bibliography — 99

Abbreviations and Acronyms

ADB	Asian Development Bank
AfDB	African Development Bank
APEC	Asia-Pacific Economic Cooperation
ASEAN	Association of Southeast Asian Nations
CCAFS	Climate Change, Agriculture and Food Security
CARICOM	Caribbean Community
CARIFORUM	Caribbean Forum
ccGAP	Climate Change Gender Action Plan
CEDAW	Convention on the Elimination of all Forms of Discrimination Against Women
CIAT	The International Center for Tropical Agriculture
COMESA	Common Market for Eastern and Southern Africa
COP	Conference of the Parties
CSA	climate-smart agriculture
CTE	Committee on Trade and Environment
DDA	Doha Development Agenda
DANIDA	Danish International Development Agency
EAC	East African Community
EASSI	East African Sub-Regional Support Initiative for the Advancement of Women
ECOWAS	Economic Community of West African States
EPA	economic partnership agreement
EPZ	export-processing zone
FAO	Food and Agriculture Organization of the United Nations
FTA	free trade agreement
FTP	foreign trade policy

GAP	Gender Action Plan
GATS	General Agreement on Trade in Services
GATT	General Agreement on Tariffs and Trade
GCF	Green Climate Fund
GGCA	Global Gender and Climate Alliance
GHG	greenhouse gas
gNES	gendered national export strategy
GRB	gender-responsive budgeting
GTF	Gender Task Force
GVC	global value chain
ICT	information and communication technology
ILO	International Labour Organization
IMF	International Monetary Fund
INDC	Intended Nationally Determined Contributions
IPCC	Intergovernmental Panel on Climate Change
IPR	intellectual property right
ISDS	Investor State Dispute Settlement
ITC	International Trade Centre
IUCN	International Union for Conservation of Nature
IUU	illegal, unreported and unregulated
LDC	least developed country
LECB	low-emission capacity-building
LLDC	landlocked developing country
LWPG	Lima Work Programme on Gender
MDG	Millennium Development Goal
MFN	most favoured nation
MSMEs	micro-, small and medium-sized enterprises
MTS	multilateral trading system
NAFTA	North American Free Trade Agreement
NAMA	nationally appropriate mitigation action
NAP	National Adaptation Plan

NDC	nationally determined contribution
NES	national export strategy
NGO	non-governmental organisation
NORAD	Norwegian Agency for Development Cooperation
NTB	non-tariff barrier
NWFP	non-wood forest product
OECD	Organisation for Economic Co-Operation and Development
REDD	Reducing Emissions from Deforestation and Forest Degradation
REDD+	reducing emissions from deforestation and forest degradation in developing countries
RTA	regional trade agreement
SADC	Southern African Development Community
SDG	Sustainable Development Goal
SIDS	small island developing states
SLR	sea level rise
SMEs	small and medium-sized enterprises
STDF	Standards and Trade Development Facility
TISA	Trade in Services Agreement
TRIMS	Agreement on Trade-Related Investment Measures
TRIPS	Trade-Related Aspects of Intellectual Property Rights
UNCTAD	United Nations Conference on Trade and Development
UNDP	United Nations Development Programme
UNEP	United Nations Environment Programme
UNFCCC	United Nations Framework Convention on Climate Change
USAID	United States Agency for International Development
USMCA	United States Mexico Canada Agreement
WTO	World Trade Organization

Summary

Achieving sustainable development is the overarching narrative of the post-2030 development agenda and the Sustainable Development Goals (SDGs). Addressing trade issues in the context of economic development and preventing dangerous climate change[1] and its negative impacts on the lives and livelihoods of women, men and children in developing countries are critical parameters in successfully meeting the post-2030 agenda. Both trade governance and climate governance are inextricably intertwined in processes that embed commitments to promote and ensure sustainable development. Yet both systems face two sets of interrelated challenges.

First, climate change and climate variability[2] have implications for the compositions and volume of trade flows, while responses to address climate change could conflict with multilateral trade rules and processes. Adverse interactions between these two processes could undermine any number of the SDGs, such as achieving food security and promoting sustainable agriculture (SDG2), ensuring the availability of water (SDG6) and access to sustainable energy (SDG7). Second, trade growth (through expansion and intensification) and trade rules may adversely affect measures taken to address climate change, particularly mitigation strategies, as illustrated in emerging debates on energy goods and services. Hence, trade policymakers may need to enhance significantly their understanding of sustainability, and climate system decision-makers may need to tread warily with measures that may have untoward consequences in the trade area and by implication on sustainable livelihoods in trade-related sectors.

Second, both systems must contend with the development implications of their processes and the reality that neither climate management nor trade policy is gender neutral. While the different circumstances of men and women as individuals, in households, communities, the labour market and the wider economy, increasingly heighten their vulnerability to climate change, they have different abilities and capacities to respond to the impacts and risks of climate change and climate-related events. An approach to addressing these differential impacts could entail investing in stand-alone programming that addresses the structural causes of gender inequality and significantly increase aid advancing gender equality as its principal focus.

For example, men and women suffer different health effects and differences in mortality rates during climate-related extreme events.[3] Emerging studies show that women are more likely than men to die during disasters, men consume more energy than women, and women are more likely than men to suffer from the burning of biomass for energy/cooking because of high levels of black carbon.[4] Pregnant women are also extremely vulnerable to vector- and water-borne diseases linked to floods (which may increase the breeding of mosquitos and other pests[5]), which are intensified by climate change. In many cases, droughts also tend to affect women's and girls' health and nutritional status because of these groups' pre-existing nutritional deficits. While the climate change governance architecture has begun to address the gendered differences often exacerbated by the challenges of climate change, the same cannot be said in the trade and development areas. Over the past two decades, there has been a growing body of policy-relevant literature aimed at establishing the two-way interlinkage between gender and trade; that is, addressing gender equality can help to ensure benefits from trade, and trade policy and its execution can either improve or exacerbate gender inequality.[6]

Against this backdrop is a new threat to achieving the SDGs. The novel coronavirus (COVID-19) is a viral infection that emerged in China in December 2019. It had the potential to kill millions of people globally, without government action to combat its impact. The World Health Organization declared a global pandemic on 7 January 2020, calling for global action to slow the spread of the disease. This required governments to impose periodic and unpredictable 'lockdowns' of public life and the isolation or quarantine of affected people. The consequent stagnation of economies around the world has had an unprecedented negative impact on the global economy. The IMF estimates that global output will fall 3 per cent in 2020.[7] Similarly, the World Trade Organization predicts a fall in world merchandise trade of between 13 and 32 per cent in 2020.[8] Lockdowns have directly impacted sectors such as tourism, hospitality and entertainment, which rely on services supplied by people. They have also impacted sectors which rely on sophisticated global value chains across many jurisdictions, such as electronics. With a fall in global incomes, already stretched economies will find it challenging to maintain commitments to invest in the social sector, on which many of the SDGs are predicated. However, environmentalists, among others, suggest that there is a potential silver lining: that the disruption of the global economy provides an opportunity to re-think or re-align a growth agenda around a more inclusive and resilient economy, with net zero emissions by 2050 at its centre.

Inclusivity appears to be rising up the agenda, as evidenced by the growing recognition of the gender dimensions of trade at policy level, reflected in WTO member states' activity. These include the Joint Declaration on Trade and Women's Economic Empowerment,[9] launched on the side-lines of the Buenos Aires Ministerial Conference (MC 11, December 2017), an action that speaks to Member States' intentions of addressing some of the gender constraints that women face in the trade arena at the domestic level.[10] Since then, there has been considerable discourse around the relevance and applicability of gender to the assumed gender-neutral space of trade policy frameworks, and about what the proponents of the declaration regard best practices in gender and trade. At the time of writing, there remains a great deal of sensitivity about how, and if at all, the WTO, as the pre-eminent multilateral rule-making body, can or even should address gender equality and women's empowerment issues.

To date, there has been very limited integration of gender equality and women's empowerment issues into multilateral trade policies and agreements. Earlier efforts focus on integrating capacity-building for women into trade agreements and protocols such as the agreement between the EU and African, Caribbean and Pacific nations, and the EU–Mexico Global Agreement. Other early attempts included insertion of gender-related social clauses (particularly around employment discrimination). Trade unions have also raised concerns about the working conditions of women in a few custom unions and trade agreements such as the North American Free Trade Agreement (NAFTA now USMCA) and the US-Central American-Dominican Republic trade agreements. For example, there is the path-breaking role of the Chile-Uruguay (2016) trade agreement, which includes a chapter on gender, followed by the Canada–Chile (2017) agreement, but these are non-binding. Among developed countries, the EU has committed to including gender issues in trade agreements and a few of its free trade agreements have referenced this issue as well. However, no such broad-spectrum approach is adopted by other WTO members. The issue of gender and trade only began to percolate seriously at the WTO in 2017/2018, and whether or not this issue should be addressed remains a very sensitive matter among member states.

On the climate and trade front, the EU has connected trade to climate both politically and substantively by going on record as stating that it will not consider trade agreements with countries that have not ratified the UNFCCC's Paris Agreement[11]. However, there is still inconsistent and insignificant analysis of the interconnectedness of climate change and trade, and much less analysis of the interconnections of gender equality and women's economic empowerment concerns with these issues.

This publication, therefore, offers new analysis on the current state of play of gender issues in both the trade and climate arenas. It aims to inform the development of gender-responsive, cross-sectoral trade and climate strategies to support both gender machineries and national governments in ensuring coherence in their efforts to mainstream gender in both trade and climate. While acknowledging that the crossover between trade, climate change and gender is still at a very early stage, the report notes that there is no clear effective institutional framework for overseeing the triple linkage of trade, gender and climate, locally, nationally, regionally or globally. It further argues that the scope for strategic interventions to integrate gender issues and women's empowerment issues into trade and climate issues can be undertaken by a variety of institutions at the micro (individual, household and community), meso (sectoral and local government) and macro (national, regional and global) levels.

Notes

1 There is no formal definition of 'dangerous climate change'. The United Nations Framework Convention on Climate Change (UNFCCC) only makes reference to 'dangerous anthropogenic interference with the climate system', and the pre-eminent scientific body that examines these issues and assess climate risks for their policy relevance, the Intergovernmental Panel on Climate Change (IPCC), is silent on this point. But the global community has agreed to the temperature guard rail of keeping the global average temperature increases to well below 2°C (3.6°F) above pre-industrial levels and to pursue efforts to limit the temperature increase even further to 1.5°C (2.7°F). Please see Box 2.1 for definitional issues around dangerous climate change.
2 Please see Box 1.2 on the differences between climate change and climate variability.
3 The report *Reaching Out to Women When Disaster Strikes* argues that women and children are 14 times more likely to die during disasters (Soroptimist International of the Americas 2008); up to four times as many women as men are reported to have died in the 2004 Indian Ocean tsunami

(MacDonald 2005); and more women than men died during the 2003 European heatwaves (Ledrans et al. 2004). Gender differences also show that men's mortality in disaster situations is due to risk factors such as rescue operations, outdoor work (during heatwaves), and unmarried men and elderly men living alone (European heatwaves; Ledrans et al. 2004).

4   Black carbon is reported to cause as many as 2 million deaths a year, mainly of women and children (WHO 2014).
5   Global warming is linked to a rise in mosquito-borne diseases because warming creates more mosquito-friendly habitats. It is projected that warming is likely to increase the infection rates of mosquito-borne diseases such as malaria, dengue fever and West Nile virus (*Scientific American* n.d.).
6   See, for example, Higgins (2013), Carr and Williams (2010), Aguayo-Tellez (2011), Bussolo and De Hoyos (2009), Fontana (2007, 2009), Williams (2003) and Cagatay (2001).
7   https://blogs.imf.org/2020/04/14/the-great-lockdown-worst-economic-downturn-since-the-great-depression/ [accessed 25 May 2020]
8   https://www.wto.org/english/news_e/pres20_e/pr855_e.htm [accessed 25 May 2020]
9   Joint Declaration on Trade and Women's Economic Empowerment on the occasion of the WTO Ministerial Conference in Buenos Aires in December 2017.
10 A total of 120 member states of the WTO signed up to the declaration, which was shepherded by Sweden, Canada and Sierra Leone and pushed keenly by the group International Gender Champions. Many developing countries, even some that are signatories to the declaration, are, however, cautious about what this means for the WTO rule-making portfolio and how far a gender equity agenda can be pushed. Others are sceptical, suspecting that this is a 'Trojan horse' to get developing countries to agree to negotiations on a number of 'new' matters including e-commerce (declared to be a great equaliser), and to elevate the plurilateral agreement on government procurement into the multilateral framework. Meanwhile, over 164 women's rights organisations groups and feminist organisations published an open letter (December 2017) in which they raise serious concerns about how this will in fact work to empower women.
11 See for example, Mathiesen (2018).

Chapter 1

Introduction

In 2015, Commonwealth governments agreed to at least three significant global environmental and climate-related international commitments: the 2030 Agenda on Sustainable Development, the Sendai Framework on Disaster Risk Reduction, and the Paris Agreement under the United Nations Framework Convention on Climate Change.[1] These have gone through their varied processes of national approval and now must be implemented domestically. Of the numerous important components of these agreements, the SDGs, which include climate[2] and trade-related goals, focus on essential factors that are critical to the wellbeing and lives of the women, children and men of the Commonwealth: food and nutrition security, water and sanitation, health, energy, employment, entrepreneurship and sustainable livelihoods. Although trade is not a specific Sustainable Development Goal (SDG), 'international *trade* is recognised as an engine for inclusive economic growth and poverty reduction, and an important means of implementation to achieve the Sustainable Development Goals and an important means of implementation' (UNCTAD n.d.; see also Addis Ababa Action Agenda 2015, UN (2015). The SDGs, however, do identify the key priority areas relating to trade, the trade policy landscape and the World Trade Organisation (WTO) that are identified as being relevant to these activities.[3] Mostly these areas are linked to export development and promotion, and to industrial and development planning and policy.

Some goals and related targets and measures are demarcated independently and addressed by different institutions and in different governance frameworks. These include trade-related measures (the WTO and assorted free trade agreements – FTAs), environmental issues (the various environmental treaties) and climate change (the United Nations Framework Convention on Climate Change – UNFCCC). Other areas are addressed or significantly affected by actions taken in various global governance entities including the International Monetary Fund (IMF), the World Bank, the World Health Organization, and under the auspices of the UN and related agencies such as the Food and Agriculture Organization (FAO) and the International Labour Organization (ILO). Nonetheless, these goals and their targets have significant overlaps with each other and most especially with gender equality (SDG5). All these goals therefore must be managed in a coherent fashion if they are to be successfully achieved. The question remains whether the existing institutions are sufficiently equipped, in terms of mandate and organisational structures, to rationalise their responsibilities.

The global governance entities charged with managing and implementing climate agreements and trade agreements each have their own rule-making processes, governance and enforcement arrangements, but their rules and impacts will intertwine significantly on domestic economic and social conditions locally and nationally. This is especially the case for trade rules, with their strong enforcement mechanism, and climate governance, which under the Paris Agreement will promote reduction in emissions globally. The Paris Agreement committed the world to hold temperature rise substantially below 2°C (3.6°F), and individual countries to make nationally determined contributions (NDCs) and adapt themselves to climate risks and impacts. These have implications for sectoral and economy-wide issues including the production of and trade in goods and services.

For better or worse, the success of the SDGs and the 2030 Agenda will be affected by climate change impacts, the outcome of the Paris conference in 2015, the results of WTO trade negotiation rounds and subsequent ministerial decisions. This also includes the lack of progress on integrated development aspects as agreed in Doha in 2001 (known as the Doha Development Agenda or the Doha Round). These potential outcomes hold significant implications for women's and men's economic and social advancement in developing and small states. Noting this, the research of this report pays keen attention to the experiences of these countries in the Commonwealth, to deepen understanding of how climate change will particularly impact on their sustainable development.

It is widely recognised and accepted that women make profound and lasting contributions to economic and social development, including contributing to the production of goods and services for export, and managing the local environment and communities. However, the economic and social condition of women in developing countries is hampered by far-reaching constraints and barriers to the means of production. Some important examples are the laws and policy frameworks that entrench disenfranchisement in a number of key sectors in some countries, such as finance, oil, gas and other natural resources, and public procurement. In addition, women are not well represented in leadership and decision-making around issues that are critical to their daily lives and their long-term health, wellbeing and accumulation of economic assets. Thus, any shock to the economy – whether emanating from exogenous sources such as extreme weather events, or from directional shifts in trade agreements and policies that negatively or positively affect the direction and composition of exports poses significant challenges for women's and men's social and economic empowerment. This is especially the case concerning the price of imported goods and inputs, particularly those that are important for food and health security and employment/livelihoods. The data confirms this point (Antonopolos 2009; Elson 2010; Sequino 2009), with variations due to the different historical and contemporary situations of each gender by country. In addition, the undermining of local food systems, the disadvantaging of low-income nations in trade agreements and the dismantling of domestic producer supports to comply with trade regulations all contribute to these shocks.

The extent to which climate change wreaks havoc on developing countries' economies influences their ability to produce and undertake value-additive economic diversification to increase both the quality and the quantity of what they trade. Furthermore, unilateral trade measures that may be integrated into mitigation policies and strategies of developed countries have implications for developing countries' exports and overall sustainable growth paths (including attempts at economic diversification).[4]

On the positive front, the more trade rules are favourable to and help promote development, the more finance and technology transfers may be available to developing countries. This could allow them to pursue climate-resilient development and to decrease the carbon-intensity of their goods and services, both those produced for domestic consumption and those traded across national borders.

The impact of these events on women's and men's economic and social status will depend fundamentally on how gender issues[5] and women's empowerment concerns are factored into trade and development policies and into climate protection and development policies. Gendered economic and social status will also be influenced by the degree of, or lack of, coherence between the two arenas. Increasingly, the mitigation of climate change and trade are destined either to clash or to work out amenable positions that reinforce sustainable development priorities. At this juncture, it is important to analyse the points of shared vision, approaches and mechanisms as well as tools of trade and climate policies. From there we can begin to unravel the adverse impacts as well as potential opportunities and interlinkages from a gender-sensitive and gender-responsive perspective.

This situational analysis details the synergies, dissonances, points of challenges and opportunities between the trade and climate regimes. It also provides a holistic view of how to better engage policies and policy-makers to continue the acceleration of the promotion of gender equality and women's empowerment in Commonwealth regions.

The main intent is to identify in broad strokes the climate and trade issues that are pertinent to gender equality and women's empowerment in the current global discussion, and to present a new conceptual framework to link these two areas holistically. This work also seeks to examine the scope of these emerging issues, singly and in combination, in order to suggest pathways for further case studies. The aim of these case studies would be to provide a more in-depth view of the issues as they affect the lives of women and men in the Commonwealth as well as how these matters are being addressed at national, regional and global policy levels.

The analysis is presented in four parts. Chapter 2 outlines the context and background of the study including a brief exploration of the features and highlights of sustainable development relevant to operationalising the nexus of gender issues, trade and climate change. It ends with an overview of the linkages between trade and climate at key sectoral levels (agriculture, fisheries, forestry, energy and tourism) that are important for gender equality and women's empowerment in the context of sustainable development. Chapter 3 explores the trade and climate policy landscape, including trade and climate governance linkages, and highlights how gender issues are taken on board in each domain. Chapter 4 looks at strategic interventions focused on integrating gender issues and concerns into both climate change policies and trade policies. It examines, through indicative case studies and examples, institutional national, regional and global approaches to integrating gender into trade and into climate policy. Chapter 5 rounds off the paper with recommendations for the way forward for research, policy and actions.

As this report will utilise many terms that may be unfamiliar to the reader, a short glossary on gender and climate change terminology is presented at the outset in Boxes 1.1 and 1.2.

Box 1.1 Gender terminology and gender policy approaches

Sex means the physiological characteristics of male and female (men and women).

Gender is determined by society's views of the appropriate roles of and behaviours for women and men (WHO 2014). Gender norms in a given society can lead to differences between females and males in social position and power, and in access to resources and services (Muralidharan et al. 2015).

The term 'gender' as used in this report covers all gender identities: men, women and non-binary persons. As is widely noted in the literature, gender issues intersect with other challenges that might be associated with age, disability, race, ethnicity, nationality or language skills.

Gender equality (the ultimate goal): all men and women are free to develop personal abilities and make choices without limitation set by stereotypes, rigid gender roles or prejudices. Men's and women's aspirations and needs are considered valued and favoured equally. Targets toward this goal may include measures to promote:

> **Gender parity:** measures the relative equality between men and women, not just the ratio. It measures the 'quality and/or value' of the differences between the sexes.
>
> **Gender balance:** the ratio of women to men in any given situation. Gender balance is achieved when there is approximately an equal number of men and women present or participating (UNFCCC 2015).
>
> **Gender equity:** fair or equivalent treatment for men and women according to their respective needs, (rights & obligations, benefits and opportunity).

Gender mainstreaming is the global strategy for gender equality. It is 'the process of assessing the implications for women and men of any planned action, including legislation, policies or programmes, in all areas and at all levels. It is a strategy for making women's as well as men's concerns and experiences an integral dimension of the design, implementation, monitoring and evaluation of policies and programmes in all political, economic and societal spheres so that women and men benefit equally and inequality is not perpetuated. The ultimate goal is to achieve gender equality' (UN ECOSOC agreed conclusions 1997/2). Effective gender mainstreaming will require gender analysis and gender-disaggregated data for utilisation in the various programming approaches.

Gender analysis is a type of socio-economic analysis that uncovers how gender relations affect a development problem (UNFCCC 2015).

Gender-disaggregated data are data that are collected and analysed separately for women and men. This typically involves asking the 'who' questions in an agricultural household survey: who provides labour, who makes the decisions, and who owns and controls the land and other resources. Alternatively, it may involve asking men and women about their individual roles and responsibilities (UNFCCC 2015).

Gender action plan: a comprehensive framework for addressing gender issues and implementing programmes and projects. It is usually based on gender and social analyses and includes a range of strategies, activities, resources, gender capacity-building initiatives, targets and indicators for ensuring that women, along with men, participate in and benefit from all components of the project and programme (Hunt et al. 2007).

There are multiple approaches to integrating gender issues into policies and programming, including:

Gender-responsive: identifying, reflecting on and implementing interventions needed to address gender gaps and overcome historical gender biases in access to economic and social resources, policies and interventions. It can contribute to the advancement of gender equality with the aim to 'do better'.

Gender-sensitive: understanding and considering the social and cultural factors underlying sex-based discrimination, with the aim to 'do no harm'. This can also be similar to 'gender-accommodating', recognising and working around or adjusting for inequitable gender norms, roles and relationships. For example, gender-sensitive programmes are programmes in which gender norms, roles and inequality have been considered and awareness of the issues raised. Corrective actions may or may not be taken.

Gender-transformative: making gender central to the policy, programme or project. It promotes gender equality as a priority, and aims to transform unequal relations, power structures, access to and control of resources, and decision-making spheres. Programmes are said to be gender-transformative if they facilitate critical examination of gender norms, roles and relationships; strengthen or create systems that support gender equity; and/or question and change gender norms and dynamics (Muralidharan et al. 2015).

Box 1.2 Weather, climate, climate change and climate variability: how do they differ?

Weather describes current atmospheric conditions, such as rainfall, temperature and wind speed, at a particular place and time. It changes from hour to hour, day to day and maybe month to month.

Climate refers to the average of how such atmospheric conditions behave over years or decades.

Climate change means a change in climate which is attributed directly or indirectly to human activity that alters the composition of the global atmosphere and is in addition to natural climate variability observed over comparable time periods[6]. The more precise Intergovernmental Panel on Climate Change (IPCC) definition of climate change refers to any change in climate over time, whether due to natural variability or as a result of human activity.[7]

Climate variability refers to the climatic parameters of a region varying from its long-term mean, such as short-term changes in climate that take place over months, seasons and years. These may be due to non-anthropogenic or natural (internal) factors generated by the climate system itself – for example, El Niño (warming phase)/La Niña (cooling phase) oscillations, both of which drive changes in circulation, winds, rainfall and ocean surface temperatures – or external factors, 'natural forces', that are related to the presence of natural radioactive gases and aerosols in the atmosphere which perturb the radiative energy of the Earth.

Adverse effects of climate change 'means change in the physical environment or biota resulting from climate change which have significant deleterious effects on the composition, resilience or productivity of natural and managed ecosystems or on the operation of socio-economic systems or on human health

Notes

1 The 2030 agenda, which includes 17 global goals and 169 targets, was adopted by world leaders at the UN summit in September 2015. It builds on the previous Millennium Development Goals (MDGs) and is promoted as the agenda for 'people, planet and prosperity', with the goals focused on areas of critical action for this purpose. The Sendai framework and declaration were adopted at the Third UN World Conference in Sendai, Japan, on 18 March 2015. With its seven clear targets and four priority areas of action, the framework seeks to prevent new disasters and reduce existing ones. It succeeds the Hyogo Framework (2005–2015) and has a 15-year duration, until 2030. The Paris Agreement, which sets a global action plan to put the world on track to avoid dangerous climate change by limiting global warming to well below 2°C above pre-industrial levels and to pursue efforts to limit the temperature increase even further to 1.5°C (2.7°F), was adopted in December 2015 at the 21st Conference of the Parties (COP) of the UNFCCC. It entered into force on 4 November 2016 and its outcome will be implemented in 2020 and will have impacts for the foreseeable future.
2 Goal 13: Take urgent action to combat climate change and its impacts. Targets 13.a and 13.b mention mobilising $100 billion a year and operationalising the Green Climate Fund (GCF).

3. Mainstreaming Trade to Attain the Sustainable Development Goals, (2018) WTO https://www.wto.org/english/res_e/booksp_e/sdg_e.pdf pp 5–7
4. Economic diversification is generally taken as the process of producing a growing range of economic outputs. It can also refer to the diversification of defined for exports or the diversification of income sources away from domestic economic activities (e.g. income from overseas investment) (UNFCCC n.d.a).
5. Critical theorists and feminists argue that the root causes of women's economic inequality are traced to economic and patriarchal structures and social attitudes, influence the market, expectations and assumptions regarding women's role as primary caregivers without, perpetuate gender bias and discrimination in the labour force, and heavily shape attitudes towards women's rights.
6. United Nations Framework Convention on Climate Change (1992). Available from https://unfccc.int/files/essential_background/background_publications_htmlpdf/application/pdf/conveng.pdf (accessed 29 July 2019).
7. https://unfccc.int/files/press/backgrounders/application/pdf/press_factsh_science.pdf (page1). Further, The IPCC's more technical definition: Climate in a narrow sense is usually defined as the "average weather," or more rigorously, as the statistical description in terms of the mean and variability of relevant quantities over a period of time ranging from months to thousands of years. The classical period is 3 decades, as defined by the World Meteorological Organization (WMO). These quantities are most often surface variables such as temperature, precipitation, and wind. Climate in a wider sense is the state, including a statistical description, of the climate system. http://www.ipcc.ch/ipccreports/tar/wg2/index.php?idp=689

Chapter 2

The Nexus of Gender, Trade, Climate and Sustainable Development

Since at least 1987, when the World Commission on Environment and Development's *Our Common Future* explicitly and formally recognised the conflict between economic development and the environment, sustainable development has been the key narrative and goal of economic and social development. The focus of development theorists, practitioners and governments has been on how developing countries can pursue economic development in an environmentally sustainable way. This requires that the production and accumulation of capital assets, knowledge base and institutions be re-oriented not only to yield goods and services for the current generation but to do so in a way that also protects the welfare of future generations. Thus, development should proceed on a pathway that seeks to maintain biophysical life support systems, protect biodiversity and involve the widest possible participation of women and men. These pathways should also take into account the factors that are important for the wellbeing of girls, boys and young adult males and females, when building a governance framework for the development process.

Through the MDGs, and now the SDGs in the framework of the 2030 Development Agenda process, developing countries have been working to improve health outcomes and create decent, good-quality employment for the men and women within their borders. Strategies for green growth, low-emission (or low-carbon) development have been actively sought out for their potential to accelerate this process.[1] Great emphasis has been placed upon a number of measures, for example reducing vulnerability to the impacts of climate change and climate variability and managing climate risks.[2] This includes changes in temperature and precipitation leading to droughts or agricultural losses. In addition, there is increasing focus on sudden risks including tropical storms and floods), as well as the recognition that developing countries need to diversify the baskets of goods and services they trade.

Since many countries, especially in Africa, are still reliant on agricultural production and exports, the link between agriculture, food and water and addressing climate change has become a key concern. Increased agricultural production can lead to increased trade, but it may also increase environmental emissions of methane and nitrous oxide. At the same time, increases in production of agricultural goods and products can both lessen food insecurity and, by providing more income, lead to an increase in the response strategies to build resilience in the face of climate vulnerability.

To chart a clear path towards sustainable economic growth and social prosperity, we must act now to address the adverse effects of climate change while simultaneously promoting economic and social development. This sustainability is central to measures to enable women, men and children to live healthy lives, with decent work,

> **Box 2.1 Dangerous climate change and the 1.5 to 2°C policy options**
>
> There is no formal definition of 'dangerous climate change'. The UNFCCC only refers to 'dangerous anthropogenic interference with the climate system', and the pre-eminent scientific body that examines these issues and assesses climate risks for their policy relevance, the IPPC, is silent on this point. However, UNFCCC parties adopted the 2°C danger limit under the Cancun 2010 Agreement to avoid catastrophic interference with the climate system. This was reaffirmed in the 2015 Paris Agreement, which also pledged to pursue efforts to limit the temperature increase to 1.5°C above pre-industrial levels, to significantly reduce the risks and impacts of climate change. The G7 governments have a political agreement dating from 2015 on a temperature guardrail of keeping the global average temperature rise to 2°C above the pre-industrial level. This danger limit appears to have been adopted by the scientific community to varying extents. Some scientists such as Hansen et al. (2013) have argued that the published science to date shows that above 2 degrees C 'is an intolerably dangerous target to aim for … and should be avoided.' They, thus support the position of most Commonwealth countries, which are among the over 100 of the world's most vulnerable nations that have asked for the under 1.5°C policy option.
>
> The logic behind the 2°C limit is that human beings, ecosystems and human systems may not be able to tolerate temperature increases above 2°C. Humans and ecosystem have been doing well for the last 10,000 years, which have been fairly warm, but, with temperatures rising since the late 1880s, there is considerable uncertainty for ecosystems, human health and wellbeing beyond a 1°C level increase. This is based on accepting that a dangerous atmospheric concentration of greenhouse gases poses risks (measured in terms of the precautionary formula endorsed by the IPCCC: Risk = Probability × Magnitude). The risks can affect unique and threatened systems (e.g. coral reefs). Impacts of and vulnerabilities to extreme weather events (e.g. floods, tropical cyclones and other storms, and soil moisture deficit) can be unevenly distributed (e.g. among indigenous communities). The aggregate impacts can affect GDP, economic development, society and ecology. Furthermore, there are risks of large-scale singularities: systems that behave in an irregular and unpredictable way leading to rapid, large and unexpected climate change impacts on local, regional and global scales, e.g. a large partial deglaciation of the Greenland ice sheet or the melting of the Greenland and West Antarctic ice sheets (IPCC 2007).

dignity and the opportunity to attain the full realisation of their human potential in the global economy. Sustainable trade is a core aspect of the engine of such national and global growth. Sustainable development, climate change, trade and managing the economy are therefore inextricably intertwined.

Climate change is arguably the most significant threat to sustainable development. It can potentially push millions of women, men and children into poverty because of its impact on agriculture (soil and yields), water (quantity and quality), health (diseases and new pests), housing and infrastructure (losses and damage), including what is necessary for the production of goods for domestic consumption and for trade. Similarly, adverse shocks to the trade system can have dramatic negative consequences for developing countries given the high dependence of developing countries' economies, particularly those of small states, on the export of goods and services to generate income, employment and livelihood opportunities and hence to promote sustainable development.

Addressing climate change presents opportunities that may create employment and help with poverty eradication, perhaps through the creation of innovative products that attempt to curb the effects of climate change on various sectors or communities, or products that can enhance developing countries' export profiles. For example, since the early 2000s, China has become a major player in the renewable energy sector, exporting Chinese solar photovoltaic cells and modules, and is poised to become a big exporter of wind turbines (Liu and Goldstein 2013; Shen and Power 2017). The country has also become poised to produce significant exports after capturing its rapidly growing home market. Furthermore, Brazil has become an important exporter of ethanol and biodiesel.

The equitable and sustainable growth of international trade presents multiple pathways to stimulate development. When the positive effects of both these important phenomena occur simultaneously, economies may prosper. However, if these factors interact negatively, this could undermine the achievement of sustainable development across many areas, and in total.

2.1 Gender and sustainable development

Proven synergy between women's empowerment and economic, social and environmental sustainability includes women's involvement in decision-making in the allocation of public resources and investment, increased labour market participation, and access to and control of growing streams of income. Women's involvement in investment and resource allocation can lead to the prioritisation of investment in human capital (i.e. education of healthier girls and boys; Hoddinott and Haddad 1995; Bloom et al (2017) as well as to women's increased participation in the labour force and their contribution to both household and national income. When women have access to and control of income, there is a high impact on the health and wellbeing of children and families (UN Women 2014). Research show that increases in women's paid employment can potentially contribute to economic growth by increasing per capita income by 14 per cent by 2020 and 20 per cent by 2030 (Aguirre et al. 2012; Stupnytska et al. 2014).[3]

Some studies also argue that increases in the share of household income (own earnings or cash transfers) controlled by women tend to be spent to the benefit of children (Hoddinott and Haddad 1995; Bloom et al. 2017), thereby increasing health and the development of human capital in the service of the economy. Furthermore, if women had the same access as men to productive assets, agricultural output in 34 developing countries would increase by an average of 4 per cent (UN Women 2017).

In addition, the number of undernourished people in those countries would decrease by 17 per cent (150 million fewer hungry people; UN Women 2017). Thus, gender equality and women's economic and social empowerment are critical for ensuring sustainable development. However, gender equality and women's abilities and capacities to gain more power and control over their lives is challenged by chronic underinvestment in gender equality interventions and the continuing low rates of women's participation in decision-making at all levels (household, local, national and regional; UNDESA 2005; OECD 2014a). Climate change concerns may further aggravate matters because, in the face of repeated or extreme events, policy-makers may turn their attention to climate adaptation and mitigation policies, assuming a gender-neutral interface, to the detriment of gender equity frameworks.

A gender-sensitive and gender-responsive approach to addressing climate change may help to alter this trajectory by taking into account gender-related concerns at the conception, planning and implementation phases of mitigation measures. Likewise, trade can also be an important instrument to enhance the empowerment of women by reinforcing the positive contribution of gender-responsive climate policy.

2.2 Trade and sustainable development

International trade, both on the export side and on the import liberalisation side, plays an important role in economic development. Trade has been credited as being the driving force behind the strong growth performance of newly industrialised countries such as South Korea, Taiwan and Singapore as well as the now established emerging markets of Brazil, China and India. However, what is often not well stated is that cross-border trade alone has very rarely made a nation wealthy over time. Economic history reveals that, for long-term sustainable wealth and social development, countries must effectively manage their trading relationships. This is crucial in this age of rising competitiveness, persistent global trade slow-down (although there are signs of a pick-up; IMF 2018a; World Bank 2018) and stagnation in employment, both nationally and globally. A strategic approach to trade policy and trade development is crucial for developing countries to benefit from trade and to unlock any significant and sustained dividends for poverty eradication and employment creation (beyond the traditional absorption of cheap labour) and promote sustainable development.

Sustainable development is an objective of the WTO (see preamble to the Marrakesh Agreement establishing the WTO). It is argued that the WTO rules uphold the right of members to have measures to protect the environment but it must not be arbitrary or disguised protectionism.[4] In this context, the 1994 Ministerial Decision on Trade and the Environment addressed sustainable development and argued for no policy contradiction between upholding and safeguarding an open non-discriminatory and equitable multilateral trading system (MTS) and acting for the protection of the environment. Furthermore, at the institutional and operational levels, the promotion of sustainable development was entrusted to the Committee on Trade and Development, which promotes international governance on sustainable development vis-à-vis the relationship between trade measures and environment measures. Since 2001, that committee and the Committee on Trade and the Environment have both been tasked to serve as fora for identifying and debating developmental and environmental aspects of negotiations and to work to ensure that sustainable development is reflected in the discussions. This was further reinforced by the Doha Ministerial Declaration paragraph 6, which makes sustainable development an objective of the Doha Development Agenda. Trade decision-makers seem to believe that successful trade outcomes 'can help to remove environmentally harmful trade-distortionary measures and promote greater access to environmental goods and services at cheaper cost.' (WTO 2011, p. 3).

Trade, in turn, is also integral to sustainable development and underlies many of the targets of the 17 SDGs (see Table 2.1). As far back as the 1992 Rio Declaration the importance of the open multilateral trading system and the avoidance of trade protectionism was emphasised.[5] From a climate and environmental perspective, trade openness as promoted by the WTO/MTS has been argued to result in 'more efficient use of resources (production efficiency) and stimulate growth and income levels which should support conservation, sustainability and efforts to reduce poverty.' (CBD 2018). In the sustainable development context, trade is seen as the channel for green technology transfer and the enabler of easier access by developing countries to environmental goods and services[6] (UNCTAD 2014). The case is made that trade may result in higher income for countries, suggesting that countries will be better positioned financially and therefore increase their demand for clean energy. However, an analysis of the clean energy spending patterns of some high-income countries indicates that this is not necessarily the case (IEA 2017; Harrington 2016; SE4ALL 2018).

Overall, mutual support between sustainable development and international trade has been articulated and acknowledged. A well-functioning MTS is vital for sustainable development, which in turn supports the sustainable low-carbon economy that increasingly generates tradeable goods.

2.3 Gender and trade

Women in most developing countries work in sectors, such as agriculture, textile and clothing, that are not only very important for export performance but also especially vulnerable to the effects of trade liberalisation, environmental degradation and climate change. Women constitute 53 per cent to 90 per cent of workers employed in the export sector of middle-income countries (Korinek 2005). In Southern Africa, informal cross-border trade is estimated to contribute about US$17.6 billion per year to trade within the Southern African Development Community (SADC)[7] (UNIFEM 2010), and women conduct most of this informal cross-border trade (World Bank 2011; UNIFEM 2010). Many of these cross-border traders pay duties and taxes (Maimbo et al. 2010) and contribute significantly to food security and importantly food justice[8] in the region (notably in Burundi and the Democratic Republic of the Congo), most especially during the 2008 financial crisis (UNIFEM 2010). However, these small-scale traders are vulnerable to bribery, harassment and physical attacks at border points (World Bank 2011). In addition, women are more vulnerable than men to shocks emanating from the trade sector and climate change (and increasingly the combined effects of both). Empirical evidence shows that in some cases, e.g. Chile, trade liberalisation can generate a greater adjustment burden for women (Levinsohn 1999; Tejani and Milberg 2010). Levinsohn, for example, found that the gross re-allocation rates tend to be higher for women than men.[9]

Gender issues and women's empowerment concerns are therefore central to and inextricably intertwined with issues of the impact of trade expansion and trade intensification on decent work and wages, including gender wage gaps, and the potential of female- (and male-) owned micro- and small businesses to scale up significantly to realise sustainable livelihoods and a life with dignity. These issues have been the persistent concerns of gender and women's rights activists, academic researchers and policy-makers working on international trade and development from a feminist perspective. This activism has ebbed and flowed over the last 20 years, but significantly weakened in the mid-2000s.

Into this breach came an increase of interest from international organisations such as the Commonwealth Secretariat, the International Trade Centre (ITC, focusing on women's entrepreneurship), the World Bank, the Organisation for Economic Co-operation and Development (OECD), UN Women (primarily in its earlier formation as UNIFEM) and the United Nations Conference on Trade and Development (UNCTAD). While much of the work of many of these institutional players has been sporadic and, at times, seemingly driven by negotiations or by thematic demands in publication cycles, UNCTAD's work on trade and gender has been consistent, focused and ongoing.[10]

However, there are some uncertainties about the benefits or presumed gains from trade in the light of ongoing upheavals in international political economy. These include concerns about climate change challenges, the WTO's stalled Doha Development Agenda and the rise of mega trade blocs. Developed countries have also been pushing for plurilateral agreements, such as the Agreement on Government Procurement and the Trade in Services Agreement (TISA, now defunct). There is also currently a push for plurilateral agreement on e-commerce, which could encapsulate many disciplines. However, is speculated that actors higher up in the value chain of this sector are likely to be men.[11] Such accords are further complicated by the greater extension of trade rules to behind-the-border issues (trade facilitation, competition policy and other traditional domestic regulations). These all have implications for the potential to accelerate the forward momentum on gender equality and women's empowerment.

Mega trade blocs such as the Free Trade Area of the Asia Pacific, the Trans-Pacific Partnership (now the Comprehensive and Progressive Agreement for Trans-Pacific Partnership, after the USA did not sign up), the Transatlantic Trade and Investment Partnership, and the Regional Comprehensive Economic Partnership (still under negotiation[12]), the African Continental Free Trade Area (soon to enter into force[13]), among others, are generating changes in the global trade and investment landscape. According to many economists, these mega blocs have a dual character: they are both trade agreements (focused on reducing barriers to selling goods and increasingly services) and production-sharing agreements (focused on the further internationalisation of the global value-chain production processes, which deepen global integration). These entities also push for deeper service liberalisation, WTO + intellectual property rights and investment provisions. More and more, these mega regional trade and economic blocs, not the WTO, are seen as the main loci of global trade governance.

The push by developed countries for rapid deepening of trade and investment liberalisation poses opportunities and challenges for developing countries now and in the future. Deepened liberalisation has implications on many fronts, including employment, business growth and sustainability, government revenues, healthcare, and access to basic social and infrastructural services. Given these unfolding realities, increasingly many explicit questions are being raised about trade as a tool for the economic empowerment of women.

As noted by a recent joint IMF, World Bank and WTO paper, 'trade is leaving too many individuals and communities behind, notably in advanced economies … and adjustment to trade can bring a human and economic downside that is frequently concentrated, sometimes harsh, and has often been prolonged' (IMF et al. 2017, p. 4). The report goes on to argue that trade can negatively affect groups of workers and some communities, and that competition from imports can have harsh impacts. Ultimately, the report argues that the right policies can benefit and uplift those who have been left behind. Such policies can ease adjustment to trade and strengthen overall economic flexibility and performance. The IMF et al. point to the importance of phasing in liberalisation to help to avoid labour market bottlenecks and congestion, and to buy time to put in place domestic mitigation measures, including temporary import safeguards. Mitigating policies to address negative trade impacts, they argue, could be bolstered by international cooperation that fosters soft law provisions including (1) trade agreements, (2) standards in regional trade arrangements that consider local conditions, and dialogue and cooperation on macroeconomic policies, and (3) the role of supportive domestic policies. This recognition and the recommended actions include some measures that gender and trade activists have been calling for over the last two decades.

> **Box 2.2 Summary of key recommendations gender and trade activists advocate to improve sustainable and equitable outcomes in global trade**
>
> Globally, gender activists have been campaigning and strategizing for decades to achieve vastly improved gender equitable outcomes for women in the economic sphere. The Gender and Trade Coalition is an example of the increased drive in recent years to have a long-term and sustainable impact, with a vision to transform global trade to be gender equitable and address the negative impact of trade rules on women's human rights. The coalition is an association of organizations and was initiated by feminist activists with experience in trade unions, academia, development policy and women's groups at national, regional and

global levels. Initiators include Action Aid, Gender and Development Network (GDN), The South Centre, Institute of Law and Economics at the university of Technology Jamaica, Trade Collective (South Africa) and the Third World Network. Some of the key principles that the GTC and others are calling for in the push for gender equitability in trade include a focus on:

1. Building capacity on gender equality and trade within governments;

2. Trade policies which affirm the primacy of governments' human rights obligation under the UN Charter and international treaties and customary laws;

3. Ensure trade agreements are consistent with and promote international human rights agreements and obligations as well as Agenda 2030;

4. Conduct gender and human rights impact assessments and take the findings of those assessments into account;

5. Make trade negotiations transparent and participatory;

6. Civil society and labour organizations advocating on trade must work more closely with women's rights organizations, taking into account varying concerns and priorities so that they hold governments to account for the impact of their policies;

7. Trade support the creation of decent work for women and sustainable industrial strategies;

8. International trade and investment safeguards women's livelihoods, land rights, food sovereignty and the natural environment.

Principles taken from:

https://sites.google.com/regionsrefocus.org/gtc/resources [specifically paper 'Making trade work for Gender Equality' – Gender and Development Network; points 5-6]

https://sites.google.com/regionsrefocus.org/gtc/unity-statement [points 1-4]

https://www.actionaid.org.uk/sites/default/files/publications/from_rhetoric_to_rights_towards_gender-just_trade_actionaid_policy_briefing.pdf [points 7-8]

Bandele, O (2015), 'An equal seat at the table: gendering trade policy.' [points 1 & 4,5]

In the recent trade rule-making and policy environment, the emphasis has been on micro-, small and medium-sized enterprises (MSMEs),[14] e-commerce and the digital economy. At times, it seems that MSMEs are perceived as the 'magic bullet' of the approach to gender. However, they are not such a panacea. MSMEs, particularly women-owned MSMEs, are often most detrimentally affected by the hard fault-lines of trade agreements: national treatment and most favoured nation (MFN) principles. Women-owned MSMEs constitute a large proportion of MSMEs and their goods are often supplanted by cheap imports that come with trade liberalisation. Women-owned MSMEs would also tend to benefit the most from preferential terms for trade finance and other support services such as export subsidies,[15] which are prohibited by trade restrictions that limit or discourage government support to local enterprises (ILO 2015).[16] Furthermore, as the ILO noted in the same report, female farmers are also more likely to be adversely affected by standards and other technical barriers to trade.

Women in developing countries also face negative differential consequences of trade provisions that impinge on public services and public procurement (often called the two Ps). Public services can play an important role in the distribution of unpaid care work, which women tend to undertake in disproportionate numbers. Hence, a too restrictive approach that limits governments' ability to provide these services is detrimental to women. Public procurement is also a means that governments use to deal affirmatively with historically disadvantaged and discriminated-against groups of persons, particularly women, minority groups (or majority groups, in the case of South Africa), persons living with disability and indigenous groups. Women also make up a disproportionate share of these disadvantaged categories. Therefore, feminists emphasise intersectionality; recognising that women may be disadvantaged vis-à-vis their multiple identities, including class, race, ethnicity, culture, age and health-related disabilities.

Agreements that further liberalise services may increase unpaid care and will add to women's burden. In addition, if user fees are routinely implemented in areas related to caring services, this can further deepen women's poverty (including time poverty). Worldwide, the inefficiency and failure of previously privatised public utilities, which has resulted in adverse health outcomes for various communities, has resulted in the re-municipalisation of former public utilities including in Europe, particularly in France (Marseille and Lyon), Atlanta in the USA, Buenos Aires in Argentina and Nagpur in India, among other areas. This is causing a shift towards putting essential public services, such as water, back under public management (Martinez 2013; Water Justice Project, n.d.).[17]

2.4 Climate change and sustainable development

The IPCC posits 'a dual relationship between sustainable development and climate change'. It argues that 'on the one hand, climate change influences key natural and human living conditions and thereby also the basis for social and economic development, while on the other hand, society's priorities on sustainable development influence both the GHG [greenhouse gas] emissions that are causing climate change and the vulnerability' (IPCC 2007).

The IPCC also argues that climate change 'will affect the ability of countries to achieve sustainable development goals'. (IPCC 2007). Conversely, the pursuit of those goals will in turn affect the opportunities for, and success of, climate policies.

Table 2.1 Gender, trade and the SDGs

SDGs and gender	SDGs and trade
Goal 5: Achieve gender equality and empower all women and girls 5.1 End all forms of discrimination against all women and girls everywhere 5.2 Eliminate all forms of violence against all women and girls in the public and private spheres, including trafficking and sexual and other types of exploitation 5.3 Eliminate all harmful practices, such as child, early and forced marriage and female genital mutilation 5.4 Recognize and value unpaid care and domestic work through the provision of public services, infrastructure and social protection policies and the promotion of shared responsibility within the household and the family as nationally appropriate 5.5 Ensure women's full and effective participation and equal opportunities for leadership at all levels of decision-making in political, economic and public life 5.6 Ensure universal access to sexual and reproductive health and reproductive rights as agreed in accordance with the Programme of Action of the International Conference on Population and Development and the Beijing Platform for Action and the outcome documents of their review conferences 5.a. Undertake reforms to give women equal rights to economic resources, as well as access to ownership and control over land and other forms of property, financial services, inheritance and natural resources, in accordance with national laws 5.b Enhance the use of enabling technology, in particular information and communications technology, to promote the empowerment of women 5.c Adopt and strengthen sound policies and enforceable legislation for the promotion of gender equality and the empowerment of all women and girls at all levels	**Goal 8:** Promote sustained, inclusive and sustainable economic growth, full and productive employment and decent work for all 8.a. Increase Aid for Trade[18] support for developing countries, in particular least developed countries, including through the Enhanced Integrated Framework for Trade-Related Technical Assistance to Least Developed Countries **Goal 9:** Build resilient infrastructure, promote inclusive and sustainable industrialization and foster innovation 9.3 Increase the access of small-scale industrial and other enterprises, in particular in developing countries, to financial services, including affordable credit, and their integration into value chains and markets **Goal 14:** Conserve and sustainably use the oceans, seas and marine resources for sustainable development 14.6 By 2020, prohibit certain forms of fisheries subsidies which contribute to overcapacity and overfishing, eliminate subsidies that contribute to illegal, unreported and unregulated fishing and refrain from introducing new such subsidies, recognizing that appropriate and effective special and differential treatment for developing and least developed countries should be an integral part of the World Trade Organization fisheries subsidies negotiation

The Nexus of Gender, Trade, Climate and Sustainable Development

Other related targets

1.4 By 2030, ensure that all men and women, in particular the poor and the vulnerable, have equal rights to economic resources, as well as access to basic services, ownership and control over land and other forms of property, inheritance, natural resources, appropriate new technology and financial services, including microfinance

2.3 By 2030, double the agricultural productivity and incomes of small-scale food producers, in particular women, indigenous peoples, family farmers, pastoralists and fishers, including through secure and equal access to land, other productive resources and inputs, knowledge, financial services, markets and opportunities for value addition and non-farm employment

2.4 By 2030, ensure sustainable food production systems and implement resilient agricultural practices that increase productivity and production, that help maintain ecosystems, that strengthen capacity for adaptation to climate change, extreme weather, drought, flooding and other disasters and that progressively improve land and soil quality

3.7 By 2030, ensure universal access to sexual and reproductive health-care services, including for family planning, information and education, and the integration of reproductive health into national strategies and programmes

3.8 Achieve universal health coverage, including financial risk protection, access to quality essential health-care services and access to safe, effective, quality and affordable essential medicines and vaccines for all

Goal 17: Strengthen the means of implementation and revitalize the global partnership for sustainable development

17.10 Promote a universal, rules-based, open, non-discriminatory and equitable multilateral trading system under the World Trade Organization, including through the conclusion of negotiations under its Doha Development Agenda

17.11 Significantly increase the exports of developing countries, in particular with a view to doubling the least developed countries' share of global exports by 2020

17.12 Realize timely implementation of duty-free and quota-free market access on a lasting basis for all least developed countries, consistent with World Trade Organization decisions, including by ensuring that preferential rules of origin applicable to imports from least developed countries are transparent and simple, and contribute to facilitating market access

17.13 Enhance global macroeconomic stability, including through policy coordination and policy coherence

17.14 Enhance policy coherence for sustainable development

17.15 Respect each country's policy space and leadership to establish and implement policies for poverty eradication and sustainable development

According to Gholizadeh Nojehdeh (2017), there are three dimensions to the threats of climate change to sustainable development. The first includes climate change effects on human development, prosperity and health, which impede progress towards the SDGs. The second involves the spill-over effect of developed countries' policies to address climate change on developing countries. The third concerns the feedback effects of adaptation and mitigation actions undertaken by developing countries to address climate change.

On the first dimension, it is now widely recognised that extreme weather events have serious consequences for human development, prosperity, health and poverty eradication in the countries that are experiencing these events. In the long run, this can impede progress towards the SDGs.

The pervasive effect of climate change on agriculture in arid and semi-arid countries as well as tropical and subtropical countries is to decrease agricultural yields and create or compound water scarcity or water stress, all of which will have direct consequences for trade and long-term growth. Climate change and climate variability are already adversely affecting the lives of countless millions of men, women, boys and girls in Africa, Asia, the Caribbean, Latin America and the Pacific. Over the last 25 years, Africa, for example, has experienced twice as many weather-related disasters – including floods and droughts – as other regions of the world. It has also had the highest rate of mortality from droughts. Between 2011 and 2012, drought-driven famine killed 0.6-2.8 persons per day. Thousands of African women, children and men died in the East African drought, including 260,000 in Somalia. Asia is experiencing more rainfall due to climate change impact on the seasonal monsoons (Loo et al., 2015). This contributes to flooding especially in cities (Asia has many cities that have suffered considerable losses as a result of floods, for example Mumbai, Chennai, Surat and Kolkata in India, and Bangkok in Thailand) and affects the lives of more than 1 billion inhabitants. Summer monsoons affect water resources, agriculture, economics, ecosystems and human health throughout South Asia.

Variability in rainfall patterns, rainfall shortage and droughts affect water resources, causing wells to dry up, increasing impurities in water, hampering access to safe drinking water and threatening food supplies. On the other hand, the increased intensity and frequency of rain that is associated with tropical storms and cyclones brings more water than can reasonably be managed in a specific time frame, resulting in overburdened ecosystems and placing undue stress on biophysical resources. In addition, extreme weather events such as floods, cold spells, heatwaves and storms often have direct and negative effects on the health and wellbeing of individuals, households and communities devastatingly. Closed schools, businesses, markets, and health care clinics and limitations on various government services are only some of the results of these extreme events that result in delays, losses, and damage, thereby retarding social and economic development.

On the second dimension, policies implemented by developed countries to address climate change may have adverse consequences on developing countries. Such policies aimed at reducing emissions growth may negatively affect growth in developing countries, thus slowing down international trade and financial flows and affecting commodity prices. This may also occur, for example, with policies designed to limit carbon-based production (through the imposition of carbon standards) and those intended to improve the production of biofuels and feed stock. Here again the immediate impacts are on agriculture (via the linkage between agricultural subsidies and food prices), which will adversely affect developing countries that are net food importers.

On the third dimension, the developmental effects of adaptation and mitigation activities undertaken by developing countries themselves, which may yield robust results in the longer term, can result in short-term upheavals in both broad economic activities and international trade.

In all of these cases, negative outcomes may significantly affect food and water security, and undermine prospects for employment and livelihoods. In turn, these altered circumstances can impede the successful achievement of the SDGs, most especially gender equality and women's empowerment. Again, much of this is because of the intrinsic impacts that extreme weather events associated with climate change have on the affected communities as a whole, and the impact on women's high rates of participation in and strong contributions to sectors such as agriculture, which in turn play a critical role in the international trade positions of many developing countries.

There is broad agreement that climate change will compound existing poverty (IPCC 2007, Olson et al., 2014, IPCC 2014a/b AfDB et al, 2003[19]). Women constitute the majority of the world's poor and, given pre-existing gender disparities, stand to be

---

Box 2.3 Climate change and sustainable development – the big picture

Broad impacts and consequences of climate change

Manifestations

- Higher temperatures, variability in rainfall patterns, with reduced rainfall, droughts etc.
- Global warming affecting water resources, agriculture, food security, natural resource management, biodiversity and human health.
- Lower soil moisture worsening food production challenge in Africa, with crop yield projected to decline by as much as 50 per cent in some countries by 2020.

Impacts and implications for agriculture and food security

- Shorter rainy seasons and extended dry season affecting planting and harvesting seasons and quantity and quality of harvested products.
- Reduced water supply and quality, with impacts on agriculture, human settlements and electrification processes.
- Economic impacts from loss of agricultural production, possibly more severe in low-income countries, where there may be higher prices for food and water.

Box 2.4 Snapshots of regional variations and impacts

Africa

- High levels of solar radiation (due to its location largely between the Tropic of Cancer and the Tropic of Capricorn).

- Longer, hotter and more frequent heatwaves (which affect crop production and yields).

- Heightened vulnerability of low-income African countries to desertification, hunger, mortality rates, migration and conflict.

The 2007 IPCC assessment report, chapter on Framing Issues (Halsnaes, K., et al (2007) estimated decline in rain-fed agricultural crop yields by 50 per cent for some African countries by 2020 or the middle of the century. There will be some variation between regions and crops in the degree of reduction of yields. With respect to regional variation, the IPCC (2014) highlights yield reduction of 22 per cent for SSA, with 30 per cent or more reduction for South Africa and Zimbabwe. East African maize grown at high levels of elevation may also benefit from warming (Niang et al., 2014). Likewise, other crops such as cassava and peanuts may experience positive effects, at least up to 2030 (Niang et al. 2014). In general, however, many major crops such as wheat and beans are vulnerable to warming and other climate-related effects. A net decline in food production may also result from decrease in rainfall, or variations and changes in seasonal timing and intensity. Torrential rain and hailstorms also affect cereal production, resulting in crop loss and disease infestations affecting whole plant varieties. These climate factors will compound the disadvantages of female small-scale farmers who are already facing limited access to seed, fertiliser and credit.

Asia

- Climate change augments hydrological cycles and increases rainfall.

- Annual mean increase in precipitation will be about 3 per cent by 2020 and 7 per cent by 2050.

- This results in water stress and drought that will, in turn, affect rice growing and lead to a general decrease in yields in agricultural trade and slow economic growth.

Small island developing states

- Sea level is predicted to rise between 0.4 and 0.8 metres by the end of the century around the Pacific islands and up to 1 or 2 metres in the Caribbean region.[20]

- Storms and hurricanes are predicted to occur with increasing frequency and intensity including a rise in Category 4 and 5 storms.

- Rising sea levels will exacerbate inundation, erosion and other coastal hazards, threatening infrastructure and people's lives.

The rise in sea levels also presents serious implications for freshwater sources due to possible salt water intrusion into ground water supply. Storms will also contribute to potential contamination of fresh water; as salt water inundations may lead to compromised water quality.

Caribbean

- The Caribbean has seven of the 36 water-stressed nations in the world and, as in numerous African countries, many farmers are also dependent on rain-fed agriculture.
- Intensity and frequency of droughts and severe flooding will increase.
- Drought-like events including low water availability will increase and there will be more seasonal droughts.
- The islands will also experience continuing water challenges, leading to increases in food production costs and corresponding food prices.
- The region is also vulnerable to other climate hazards.

Pacific

- Pacific islands are vulnerable to various climate hazards including typhoons, tsunamis, flash floods, and heat waves.
- They are likely to experience public health concerns due to consequences of floods, including water-borne diseases (e.g. in Solomon Islands).

Latin America

- Key climate change impacts include serious implications for agricultural land, perhaps associated with desertification and salination.
- Likely consequences include increased stress on food and water security resulting from decreases in freshwater and intrusions of sea water.

disproportionately negatively affected by climate change. The next two sections will explore this topic, first focusing on the gendered impact of climate change, and gender and trade, and taking a more focused look at the sectoral impacts on agriculture, fisheries, forestry, energy and tourism.

2.5 Gender and climate change

All around the world, women play significant roles in adaptation and mitigation efforts. In many countries such as India and Nepal, women's self-help networks and risk management committees help to address climate risk and support adaptation measures around livelihoods, water and sanitation, and health and education. Women are managers of land, forestry and biodiversity. For example, many indigenous women in Africa and Asia are stewards of natural resources. Many have knowledge of the wild ancestors from which current plants were derived – information that can help in developing adaptive response measures, in enhancing resilience in food crop sustainability and in medicinal plants, and in maintaining ecosystems. Women in communities often practise conservation of mangrove and other drought-resistant crops, which are important for adaptation to floods and famines and for mitigation, including in relation to deforestation and carbon dioxide emissions. Women also maintain vested interests in water management and distribution as well as in the development of clean and efficient energy technologies for both household and market production activities.

However, because of gender-specific roles and gender-differentiated access to resources, women currently suffer and will be subjected to increased challenges to their health and wellbeing. These include (1) vulnerability to water-borne diseases[21] (2) an increase in burdensome collection and carrying of water (transporting an average load of 40 pounds on the head is associated with risks of an impaired skeletal system, deformity and disability) and (3) exposure to gender-based violence incidents related to distance needed to travel further away from their dwellings to obtain wood and water.

Research documents that, as a result of climate change and climate-related events, water sources close to home have become scarce or are polluted, often owing to increased levels of salination and contamination from floods and droughts. Because they have to travel greater distances, women end up facing more human hazards such as intimidation, kidnapping, and physical and sexual assaults (Bridge 2008; CEDAW 2018; Ortiz-Barreda n.d.). Some countries across Africa (e.g. Malawi and Mozambique) and in Asia (e.g. Bangladesh) have seen a rise in early marriages of girls, exacerbating the already vulnerable status of young girls' health and wellbeing.[22] Furthermore, in the event of catastrophic climate-related events, governments are likely to reallocate resources to deal with emergency losses and damages. This is likely to mean that certain public sector social programmes will see their funding diverted and targeted programmes such as measures to enhance girls' education and capacity-building for women's small and medium-sized enterprises (SMEs) will be put on hold. Broader objectives such as gender-sensitive public transport options or more accessible and safer feeder roads for all may fall by the wayside. These are but a few of the ways in which climate change can pose obstacles to women's economic and social advancement.

Climate strategies that call for radical emission reductions and societal transformation will affect men and women differently. Among the issues that climate protection policies must tackle are public transport, accessible and affordable sources of clean energy for individuals, households and businesses; responsibility for energy-efficient production and for household goods; waste management; and altering consumption patterns. Under the Paris Agreement, developing countries have undertaken commitments to reduce emissions and to transition to low-carbon pathways through their nationally appropriate mitigation actions (NAMAs) and nationally determined contributions (NDCs). These proposed efforts have numerous and complex implications for individuals, households, communities and firms. The proposed measures will result in different benefits and burdens for men and women, whether they are heads of households, small farmers or business owners who own and operate MSMEs.

According to the UNFCCC, 'NAMAs refer to any action that reduces emissions in developing countries and is prepared under the umbrella of a national governmental initiative' (UNFCCC n.d).[23] NAMAs are aimed at reducing emissions below 2020 business-as-usual levels; they are often expressed in the form of regulations, standards, programmes, projects and policies or financial incentives focused on transformational change in a particular economic sector, across sectors or economy-wide, and should contribute to domestic sustainable development. Pakistan, for example, has a NAMA that seeks increasing access to affordable, reliable and clean electricity through reducing financial and technical barriers to the deployment of distributed generation from renewable energy, in this case solar power.[24] Countries such as Ghana, Kenya and Uganda also use their NAMAs to ensure clean energy for household, community and commercial production. One aspect of Uganda's approach to its NAMA is to ensure availability of clean cooking and renewable electricity technologies to meet the electricity and cooking energy requirements of schools in a sustainable way (UNDP 2015). NAMA can also directly contribute to trade growth. For example, one dimension of Cambodia's NAMA supports energy-efficient sewing machines, washing machines, drying machines and compressors (UNDP 2015).

Although there has been no comprehensive gender assessment of NAMAs,[25] the International Union for Conservation of Nature (IUCN) has undertaken an examination of a subset of eight energy sector documents about NAMAs and found that seven include mentions of 'women' or 'gender' in the proposed objectives or outcomes of the NAMA project (Pearl-Martinez 2014). These mentions were generally made in the context of specific, gender-responsive activities, such as increasing electrification in rural households and improving the efficiency of biomass fuels for household energy uses. Increasingly, however, countries such as Georgia are developing gender-sensitive NAMAs, particularly in the area of sustainable rural energy. Such measures are specifically designed to support women living in rural areas in efforts to pursue sustainable energy transition by adapting solar water heaters and energy-efficient stoves and insulation.

While NAMAs are voluntary, NDCs are inscribed commitments that countries make under the Paris Agreement and are scheduled to be reviewed every five years with an expected progressive increase over time. Unlike NAMAs, NDCs have a broad scope covering adaptation, mitigation finance and technology transfer; NDCs too are to be developed and implemented in the context of sustainable development. With the coming into force of the Paris Agreement and its emphasis on gender sensitisation, NDCs – if not already gender-sensitive by the initial submission dates of 2015 – should be so under the review processes and certainly by their full implementation in 2020.

Developing countries' NDCs include potential adaptation actions as well as mitigation commitments. Many countries also discuss sustainable development in their NDCs.

Under the NDC commitment many Commonwealth countries have committed themselves to highly ambitious targets, dependent on each country's development needs and circumstances but not conditional on external support, to reduce emissions by from as little as 5 per cent below business as usual to as much as 81 per cent by 2030.[26] NDCs are to be revised and progressively adjusted upwards every five years. The IUCN's review of the NDCs submitted shows that 'three-fourths of sub-Saharan African parties' reference "gender" or "women" in their NDCs, making the region a global leader' (Pearl-Martinez 2014).

Macro-, meso-, and micro-level responses to climate change challenges are determined by the nature and extent of the overarching climate change policy. This includes the concepts, processes and frameworks that enable the identification and implementation of solutions in terms of the globally adopted twin strategies of adaptation and mitigation. These dual arenas are also subject to issues of gender biases and gender inequalities inherent in the global, regional, national and local economies. Both at the economy-wide and at the sectoral level, trade has the potential to leverage some of the beneficial effects of climate policies to support climate risk reduction as well as to decrease vulnerabilities. In order for this to occur, however, awareness needs to be raised about how trade empowers or does not empower men and women. Trade and climate have powerful sectoral and cross-sectoral linkages that can support gender equality and sustainable development. The next section explores three key sectors that are important for sustainable development and for men's and women's lives and livelihoods. The approach is, first, to situate the sector in the global context and, second, to highlight the role and contribution of women in that sector in the context of the climate change and trade liberalisation nexus.

2.6 Interlinkages between trade and climate at sectoral levels – implications for gender equality and women's economic empowerment

Climate change has broad economy-wide impacts but also specific sectoral and cross-sectoral impacts for developing countries' economies and the lives and livelihoods of the men, women and children within those economies. The impacts include multiple damages to infrastructure with implications for economic growth and trade, and losses and damage to resources and properties, which contribute to displacement, migration and conflicts. Specific economy-wide effects of climate change include hampered potential growth, increased cost of rehabilitation and diverting funds from development, and the cross-sectoral impacts on employment, production and reduced government revenues from decreased productivity of sectors such as agriculture, forestry and fisheries. The challenge for a large proportion of women and men is fourfold: rising water scarcity and shortage, food insecurity, loss of employment and, ultimately, loss of lives.

Climate change has economic and trade implications for climate-sensitive sectors such as agriculture and fisheries. The remainder of this section will focus on exploring these effects and their gender implications.

2.6.1 Agriculture, trade, climate change and sustainable development – gender dimensions and implications

The agriculture sector is one of those most susceptible to climate change impacts. The sector has a two-fold relationship with climate change and sustainable development. Agricultural production is dependent on fossil fuels and involves the cutting of forests and grasslands for farming. These activities contribute to rising GHGs and desertification. At the same time, the rising incidence of extreme weather events (rainfall variability, droughts and floods) undermines agricultural production by decreasing the fertility of agricultural land and undermining the utility of low-potential land (FAO 2009). Climate change contributes to changes in yield patterns and to destruction of crops that are not flood or drought resistant.[27]

In addition to heightening crop sensitivity and susceptibility to extreme weather events, climate change also contributes to water scarcity issues and the rise of pests and diseases. Rising temperatures lead to more growth and/or shifting of mosquito habitats, while floods and increased precipitation promote new mosquito breeding grounds.[28] These developments lead to various consequences for food production, food security, agricultural trade and gender equality. In many regions, such as Africa and South Asia, the lives and livelihoods of women are 'tied to the natural resource base' i.e., water resources, agriculture, aquaculture, biodiversity, land use and land use change. (Williams 2015). In these countries, as well as in the Caribbean and other small island states, rising sea levels have implications for women's and men's access to and control over essential basic needs, such as food, water and shelter. These short- and long-term impacts of climate change incur additional challenges for men and women in their multiple and dynamic relationships with agriculture, including better risk planning and enhanced adaptation actions with the attendant financing and technological costs.

Gender and agriculture

Women participate actively in sustainable agriculture and water uptake for family and community life, on their own account as well as through working on family and other types of farms., Women are 43 per cent of the agricultural workforce worldwide and over 50 per cent in Africa and Asia (Nellemann et al. 2011). In India, women undertake 4.6 to 5.7 times as much agricultural work as men. In Nepal, the proportion is even more skewed, with women carrying out 6.3 to 6.6 times as much agricultural work as men (ICIMOD 2009, cited by Nellemann et al. 2011). Women make up more than 40 per cent of the agricultural labour force in the Sahel (for example Burkina Faso, Chad, Mali, Mauritania and Niger) and play a critical role in improving food security and nutrition (UN Women 2017).

It is now a stylised fact that women farmers have significantly less access than men to arable land, information, finance and agricultural inputs and technology.[29] Women are also more likely than men to be in subsistence agriculture. Men tend to benefit more in commercial agriculture and agroprocessing.[30] Hence, female farmers are more vulnerable than male farmers to climate shocks. UN Women argues that, not only do women lack access to land, markets and finances, they are also marginalised in the type and level of agricultural activities they can engage in, which perpetuates their poverty. Patriarchal attitudes and norms are at the root of this discrimination (UN Women 2017).

Agriculture is important for women in developing countries, particularly in Africa and Asia, because of its links to food security and nutrition and also for employment and livelihoods, through domestic as well as international trade.

Several analysts (for example Wedderburn and Grant Cummings, 2017) have identified at least four dimensions of food security with respect to agriculture sector vulnerabilities: (1) food availability, food accessibility, food utilisation and stability of food systems (state of farmlands, roads, water for irrigation); (2) farming as a sustainable livelihood for women and families; (3) women's role in decision-making in agriculture, on commodity boards, etc.; and (4) equitable access to technology and other training and technical support services, for both women and men.

The authors also note that women's vulnerability in agriculture is directly related to the constraint and lack of shared responsibility for care of families. In addition, women and men farmers throughout rural Africa, Asia, and the Caribbean require the key asset land as a means of establishing and maintaining sustainable livelihoods. This is the basis on which these rural inhabitants can further household and business development. Women in these countries who lack adequate care support from men and governments find themselves constrained from creating sustainable livelihoods for themselves and their families. This remains a central and difficult challenge for women farmers of all ages. (Wedderburn and Grant Cummings, 2017).

Climate change has intensified this situation. Given the alarming impact of climate change on the social and economic wellbeing of rural men and women, there is an increasing trend towards sustainable agriculture and its integrated approach, so-called climate-smart agriculture (CSA)[31]. Sustainable agriculture is grounded in agro-ecology and focuses on the protection of traditional seeds and varieties. It aims to upscale traditional knowledge and practices that reinforce climate-resilient varieties of plants and methods for soil protection and enhancement. This approach draws deeply on women's knowledge and offers ways to enhance and sustain the income-earning opportunities of women and men in rural and farming communities.

CSA means different things to different people and/or institutions. In general, it seems to have three important pillars: (1) increasing productivity and incomes without damaging the environment; (2) enhancing adaptation by strengthening local communities' resilience and capacities; and (3) mitigation, by reducing and/or removing GHG emissions through responsible farming, soil management and afforestation. At times, it appears as if CSA-predominant activities tend to favour males and medium-sized to large farming activities, and may also involve a high degree of carbon-offsetting activities.

Trade and agriculture links

Agricultural trade is also an area of economic growth for developing countries. Agricultural business trade (and its many subsectors)[32] is a driver of climate change and holds potential for reducing vulnerability to climate change. Trade can also promote agro-industry growth as it increases the demand for agro-industry products (e.g. processed food, cut flowers and other non-traditional exports) and the level of agro-industry development.

Women are very involved in the production of goods traded on global markets, as farmers, wage workers or intermediaries (processing or selling products) at every node of the value chain (UN Women 2017; Gammage et al. 2009). They are also in demand as labour input for the fastest-growing area of agricultural trade: fresh fruits and vegetables.[33] In Africa and Asia, women predominate in both subsistence and commercial agriculture. This includes involvement in both staple crops and high-value traditional products (for which new uses and new global markets are being found). It also concerns non-traditional agricultural products such as shrimps, nuts and seeds (e.g. sunflower and other crops, which are now being adopted thanks to their resilience to drought in particular locations). At the same time there has been a shift in women's participation because, in general, small and independent famers encounter obstacles to producing many of the newly traded crops. Therefore, many women are working as labour inputs to global value chains (GVCs) and in off-farm employment producing non-traditional agricultural exports (such as horticultural and floricultural items),[34] leading to rising migration (of both men and women) from rural areas as trade expands. Increasingly, women are being incorporated into trade-related activities such as processing and packaging of agricultural exports (Kabeer 2003; van Staveren et al. 2007).

While the combined effect of climate impacts and trade expansion adjustment means that some women farmers now working as labourers in non-traditional agricultural export-related businesses, it also means that remaining women farmers are being pushed increasingly towards less fertile land. In some areas (for example in the Philippines), some women have been displaced into tourism-related zones and forced to take up jobs in domestic work or in prostitution. Research shows that medium-sized farms, (often owned by men) are better able to compete, and, in many cases, the commercialisation of traditional crops formerly produced by women is now being taken over by men. This is happening with groundnuts in Zambia, rice in Gambia and leafy vegetables in Uganda (FAO 2018; Dey 1981).

2.6.2 Fisheries, trade, climate change and sustainable development – gender dimensions and implications

Fisheries, including aquaculture and post-harvest processing along with related services, are part of the global seafood industry.[35] Industrial aquaculture is the most successful segment of the seafood industry in terms of production, employment and growth, and in 2012 38 per cent of fish products worldwide were exported.

Climate change and fisheries

Fisheries are important for food security and sustainable development in developing countries, taking Bangladesh as just one example.[36] A major long-standing problem in the sector is the persistent challenge of overfishing, illegal, unreported and unregulated (IUU) fishing, and the lack of a legally binding globally agreed framework to tackle such practices.[37] Climate change and climate variability compound these concerns. Rain is increasingly irregular and unpredictable, causing seasonal variability of water flows in rivers, worsened riverbed siltation, and increased seasonal salinization of water and soil (Mohammed and Uraguche 2013; Cheung et al. 2013). Storms, droughts, salination, coastal erosion, sea level rise and freshwater shortages all have negative consequences for coastal communities. Increased severe weather events (cyclones and floods) cause high levels of loss in aquaculture systems, affecting household income and women's time and earnings. The indirect effect is that women have less access to money and less food, so they end up with smaller amounts of essential vitamins and minerals in their diets (USAID and Comfish 2012).[38] Fisheries are also a key source of livelihood for millions of women and men although, at the level of international trade in the sector, women are not well represented at the higher-value components. This point is explored further in the following subsection, on gender and fisheries. Women are involved in outsourced processing in developing countries, such as tuna canning; they also work in export-processing zones (EPZs) where significant fish processing takes place (for example in Uganda along Lake Victoria).

Fisheries and post-harvest processes include preparing inputs and fishing gear, offloading fish from vehicles, selling to and by wholesalers, processing and packaging. The fisheries sector is highly capital intensive, requiring trawlers and large seiners, and is dominated by men. About 540 million persons depend on fisheries and aquaculture as a source of nutrition (protein) and income (FAO 2012). Some 120 million persons work in the capture fisheries and post-harvest industry and its value chains. Almost half of these (47 %) are women, 'often poor women' (NORAD 2016). Globally, one in two seafood workers is a woman (Monfort 2015). In Bangladesh, women tend to dominate in subsistence, artisanal and industrial fishing.[39] They comprise 70 per cent of the total workforce; 72 % in Asia, 20 % in Africa, 24 % in the EU, 13 % in Norway and 10 % in Chile (Monfort 2015; FAO, 2014). Overall in the sector, though women are said to be efficient, they are invisible, operating at the lower end of the value chain, receive low remuneration (lower paid or underpaid) and are 'less endowed to face adverse external events' (Monfort 2015).

In aquaculture, approximately 38 million persons are engaged in fishing and related activities. Poor women and children procure shell sand crabs and cultivate seaweed (NORAD 2016). In small-scale aquaculture, women tend to combine housework with the business. They may work as artisanal fishers, or as traders, processors and gleaners, performing tasks such as purchasing, fingerlings, seeding fish or checking the quality of water. Some women from developed countries (USA, Canada) may work on boats but many work as processors. Up to 80 per cent of all the fish and shellfish caught by local, artisanal fishers in tropical Africa, Asia and the Pacific are cleaned, dried, smoked and marketed by women and children (Williams 2015). Women also try to undertake business in the sector. Women in some African countries (Nigeria, Guinea and Senegal) also provide financing for fishing operations. However, as is the case in other sectors, women in fisheries also generally lack access to credit.

Gender and fisheries

Women fishers and fish workers carry out 20 per cent of inland fishing, with 15 per cent directly engaged in the primary fisheries sector (FAO 2014. Women form 73 per cent of the total fisheries and post-harvest workforce in Nigeria, 72 per cent in India, 40 per cent in Mozambique and 21 per cent in China, while in Canada women tend to work in onshore family enterprises where they manage and maintain the operation (Neis et al. 1996). In the EU, women constitute 21 per cent of the fisheries workforce and play multiple roles: management (fiscal, supply sourcing), communication, bookkeeping, marketing and backup logistical support.

Monfort (2015; see also OECD 2014b; World Bank 2012b) argues that women participate in all segments of the seafood industry, including fishing, farming, trading and selling, monitoring and administration. However, in most cases, there are straightforward and pervasive gender differences in the sector. Though women are crucial to fisheries, they face specific gender constraints arising from historical socio-cultural traditions. Men work in capture fisheries, while women undertake preparation, fish processing and small-scale trade (NORAD 2016). In many countries, women dry and smoke fish. Many sell the finished products to customers in various villages by head-loading. Overall, in terms of seafood processing (fresh and frozen), women are important for processing fish products or otherwise transforming the input. Women predominate in the labour force in processing; 85.5-90 per cent of fish processors are women (World Bank et al., 2010; FAO 2012). This is the case of the west coast of Africa, where most fish processors are women performing multiple roles such as ensuring the availability of fish year-round, and preserving it (smoking and salting). They also process fresh fish and sell it locally or use it to feed their families. In Nigeria women predominate in the fresh and dried fish market. They head-load and vend fresh fish to household markets. In Cambodia 80 per cent of the workforce are women producing fish sauce. In Solomon Islands 26 per cent of the fisheries workforce is female. In Fiji Islands 90 per cent of cannery workers are women (Lambeth et al. 2014, cited by Monfort 2015). In India, in some regions women are predominant among workers processing shrimps (70 per cent of the total fisheries labour force). These women receive low pay and no welfare or social security (Monfort 2015; OECD 2014b; World Bank 2012).

Men tend to use more capital and equipment in their work. Women work with little equipment and less capital. Many who operate in the intertidal zone,[40] shallow water or reefs use knives, wooden or metal sticks, nets or traps, bags or baskets, and kerosene or gas lamps (at nights) to glean molluscs, crustaceans, small fish and algae to provide protein and generate income for their families and communities. Subsistence fishing in particular has been identified as a source of protein for families. For example, women in Samoa are responsible for collecting most marine bivalves and other invertebrates, which account for 20 per cent of the per capita seafood consumption (Lambeth et al. 2014).

Women also work in pre-harvesting activities: mending of nets, gathering of bait and preparation of food for fishing trips. Women's post-harvest work often involves carrying fish from shore, sorting and cleaning fish, processing activities (drying, freezing, smoking and fermenting), marketing, sales and trading. They also do unpaid work supporting the fishing operation: childcare, managing households. Women often have specialised knowledge of the fish species they catch, particularly with regard to habitats and ecosystem change.

Box 2.5 Fish and the climate change–trade nexus: the case of Senegalese women

In Senegal, 90 per cent of fisheries seafood processors are women; that is, approximately an estimated 40,000 women work as fish processors, drying, salting and smoking fresh fish. Yet women make up less than 5 per cent of the members of governance bodies and they lack access to capital, resources and information (Kwan 2017). In processing facilities, women are less paid than men for the same jobs, so there are significant income disparities. At the same time, women face serious challenges to their lives and livelihoods. Long-standing overfishing by foreign fleets, illegal fishing and climate change are making fish scarce in the region and this is having an adverse impact on processors (Benavides 2018a; Beatley and Edwards 2018). Increasingly, women from the sector are turning to the export sector to find alternative income 'in order to feed their families and maintain some degree of financial autonomy, women are better off exporting fish products to foreign markets' (Beatley and Edwards 2018; Benavides 2018a; COMFISH/USAID 2012). But this has contradictory implications for food security as a large proportion of these women and their families remain highly dependent on protein for fish for food security and wellbeing. As noted by a USAID study, 'dwindling fish stocks pose an imminent food security threat to Senegal' in terms of 'hidden hunger,' or micronutrient deficiency including lack of protein' (COMFISH/USAID 2012).[41]

In other countries (Cambodia, Congo and Thailand, for example) women fish in small boats, taking short trips in lakes and rivers. In Lao PDR, however, men and women are found to utilise motorised boats and gill nets in fishing. Nonetheless, there are still distinct gender roles: women control the boat and pull the nets, and men dive.

Like other sectors of the economy, the fisheries and aquaculture ecosystems are also affected by climate change, with implications for women's participation. Climate change affects water quality and flow, estuaries, coral reefs, mangroves and seagrass beds and thus has an impact on fish distribution (the structure and location of production) and the productivity of marine and water species. It is known that small wild fish (e.g., anchovies and sardines) are sensitive to changes in ocean conditions (FAO 2018). These are linked to aquaculture, as these small fish are often processed into fishmeal, which is then used to feed other fish as well as pigs and poultry (FAO 2018).

In addition, as pointed out by a recent FAO study, climate change creates warmer weather, which will influence the abundance and mortality rates of wild fish stocks as well as fish farming (FAO 2018). The increasing frequency of extreme weather events (cyclones and floods) is causing considerable losses in the aquaculture system in Bangladesh.

Women will be affected by these changes. Research on the sector in Bangladesh shows that women's range of livelihood opportunities might disappear if fish production decreases. Research also notes less participation of women than men in pre-harvest and post-harvest fishing activities (Uganda). Hence, adapting the fisheries sector to climate change, and to the different strategies of men and women in communities that are dependent on fisheries, is important for sustainable development. Strategies are also being put in place to enhance resilience and productivity and promote the diversification and integration of aquaculture systems. The Consultative Group on International Agricultural Research and the International Rice Research Institute are researching water management and are promoting strategies to relocate fish roads and improve fish circulation in rice fields, other vertical agricultural systems, drip irrigation and drain-harvesting water systems. Research is also being updated to increase the understanding of women's role and their participation in the sector by for example the Norwegian Agency for Development (NORAD), the Network of Aquaculture Centers in Asia-Pacific (NACA) and the FAO. The joint FAO-NORAD ecosystem approach to fisheries Nansen initiative to support the implementation of the ecosystem approach in the management of marine fisheries in developing countries, also aims to strengthen the gender dimension in strategic interventions, programmes and projects.

Fisheries: the trade–climate link

On trade and climate interconnectedness relative to fisheries, the main challenge with fisheries trade for many developing countries is the subsidies implemented by developed countries. These subsidies can exacerbate the climate impacts but, most troublingly, they impede sustainable development. In Senegal, women's livelihoods in the fishing sector are adversely affected by the alleged activities of Korean and Russian fishing companies. The activities of these companies are reported to result in loss of jobs and income for women, and displacement of local communities (Beatley and Edwards 2018).

SDG target 14.6 highlights this concern. It argues for the prohibition of certain forms of subsidies that contribute to overcapacity and overfishing, and calls for the elimination of subsidies that contribute to IUU fishing. There is ongoing discussion in the WTO about prohibiting such subsidies. A key issue for developing countries, and important for women, is special and differential treatment, since many small fishers do not contribute to overfishing and are reliant on some government subsidies. The 2017 WTO Ministerial Conference agreed to work towards the creation of disciplines (i.e., regulations) on fisheries by 2019. Such disciplines are proposed to be comprehensive and effective, to prohibit certain forms of fisheries subsidies that contribute to overcapacity and overfishing; these disciplines would eliminate subsidies that contribute to IUU fishing. This would put the WTO in alignment with SDG target 14.6, which sets a deadline of 2020 for the elimination of such subsidies in the context of special and differential treatment. Achieving this would greatly help to halt the decline in global fish stocks. It is argued that an annual 5 per cent decline in global fishing would lead to the recovery of fish stocks. This would help to bolster women's and men's livelihoods in the fisheries sector (Beatley 2018; COMFISH / USAID 2019.; World Bank 2019a).

2.6.3 Forestry, trade, climate change and sustainable development – the gender dimensions

Forests are important in the struggle against climate change; they are natural carbon sinks for carbon sequestration and so help to reduce GHGs. Forests also provide wood and non-wood products for domestic consumption and international trade (see box 2.7); nuts, fruits, resins, gum, charcoal and social and environmental services; and soil moisture that supports agriculture, fisheries, energy production, water supply and tourism. Forests in turn are affected by human economic activities such as agriculture and mining, which cut and clear forests, depleting forest cover and causing deforestation and degradation. Forests are also affected by trade policies (such as tariff and non-tariff barriers), which may accelerate or decelerate the cutting down of forests.

Forest conservation, preservation and maintenance are critical to advancing sustainable development and to the lives of countless millions of women and men who rely on forests and forest products and other ecosystem services provided by the world's forests. Yet forests are in danger, threatened by deforestation, degradation and changing land use patterns. Forests are important for SDG13 (climate change) and SDG15 (life on land). Though forestry is male dominated at the policy and decision-making level and in large-scale industrial processing, women are the main users of forests (for wood, food and medicines) in many developing countries, as discussed below.

Gender issues in forestry

Women in Africa, Asia and Latin America are noted to have knowledge of and a high degree of dependence on forests and forest products. They are often at the forefront of conservation of forests as well as managing forests, agroforests and tree genetic resources. An example is the work of the Chipko Movement in India in the 1970s. Noted for being the original 'tree huggers', these women challenged the extensive logging that was taking place in their communities. Their struggle contributed to a major reform of India's forestry laws. Also in the Asian region, the Tebtebba Foundation in the Philippines works to promote indigenous women's and men's continued access and ownership rights to natural resources. In the Latin American region, there is the long tradition of the Wangki women of Nicaragua, who work to prevent deforestation and degradation, which ensures that more carbon remains in the trees and forests and is not released into the atmosphere.

In Africa, the most famous of all, the Green Belt Movement, a Kenyan women's non-governmental organisation (NGO) at the grassroots level, began to plant trees in 1977 to tackle the problems of deforestation, soil erosion and water scarcity. Led by the Nobel laureate Wangari Maathai, the Green Belt Movement is acclaimed for having planted millions of trees, thereby also preventing deforestation and degradation and helping to preserve the soil in Kenya.

Women in forest communities can generate more than 50 per cent of their income from forests, compared with about one third for men. Yet according to researchers (such as Tinker 1994; Locke 1999; Agarwal 2001; Blessings et al. 2006; Angelsen and Jumbe 2007) women do not fare well under forestry co-management and devolution programmes or mitigation-oriented programmes. Often, changes in tree cover and loss of access to forests can therefore have a disproportionate impact on women, with indirect impacts on the livelihoods of five to ten times as many people (CIFOR 2013).

Gender issues and REDD+

Women are vital for the conservation of forests around the world (Aguilar et al. 2011). Yet an analysis by the Global Forest Coalition of the impact of market-based mechanisms such as the Reducing Emissions from Deforestation and Forest Degradation (REDD+) Plus programme and similar initiatives argues that the 'position of women within the communities was also affected, as women interests are more likely to be over-looked in commercial transactions normally closed by men (even in communities where women previously had responsibility for matters related to forests and biodiversity)' (GFC 2009, p. 7). The report further notes that women have a serious disadvantageous with monetization of forest and related products. This is so for two primary reasons. In the first case, gender-specific roles normally allocated as women' activities (childcare, household management, procuring clean water etc.) are not rewarded in monetary terms. Second, women are generally the poorest of the poor and hence among those who depend on the forest and will suffer more from the loss of the multifunctionality of forests (GFC 2009, p.7).

Women's efforts are critically important in many developing countries for sustainable forest management (reducing harvest rates and harvest damage). Gender concerns and priorities should be an essential core of initiatives designed to improve forest governance arrangements, strengthen capacities and means for forest law enforcement, encourage adoption of reduced-impact logging and strengthen forest conservation programmes. Women's and men's different constraints, challenges and opportunities to respond effectively to new opportunities must be the basis for the development of community-based small-scale forest enterprises in the area of wood and non-wood forest products (NWFPs) and improving forest fire management systems (paraphrased from UN-REDD 2009).

Unfortunately, as noted by UN-REDD 2009, 'REDD schemes do not automatically guarantee a capacity to link carbon sensitive policies with pro poor and environmental policies (for income, employment generation, for asset/rights/biodiversity preservation and for social/cultural cohesion).' However, this does not mean that gender equality outcome cannot be integrated into the policy framework prior to implementation or next based as part of outcome assessment of a result-based management framework. Since it is widely acknowledged that 'REDD induced changes to legal frameworks that regulate incentives, rights, financing options (including taxation) and practices do not necessarily ensure equitable delivery' (UN-REDD), rather it is already predisposed to transforming legal and institutional policy processes. Certainly, women's rights, particularly as they relate to the use and ownership of forests and forest related products, is an important set of rights that must be bolstered and safeguarded. Finally, gender sensitive indicators must be one of the pro-poor co-benefit indicators anchored within the REDD benefit distribution systems (UN-REDD 2009).

Unfortunately, the myths of the male farmer, the male business owner and the male head of household continue to dominate the imagination of climate change policy decision-makers (Dankelman 2002, Gennovate (2018) and Jerneck 2017). In the case of REDD programming, it is important to undertake gender and social impact assessments in order to ensure that women and indigenous groups do not lose ownership or usufruct rights to their traditional land or land to which they have historical, communal access. Great care and attention is needed to ensure that women and poor men receive their equitable share in the benefits to be derived from community resources. This can be ensured through community benefit-sharing agreements and gender-sensitive property rights arrangements. They should also be protected from disproportionately shouldering the burden of any adverse costs of projects funded under REDD and other related projects, which involve land use or land use change or the use of forests for reforestation, afforestation or for carbon-offsetting projects.

National governments should also enact appropriate regulations for private sector initiatives that have an impact on poor women's and men's access to and ownership of land, access to water and other economic resources. These regulations should include careful monitoring of the issue of resource conflicts arising from dispossession and take-over of land ('land-grabbing') from vulnerable groups with traditional usufruct access to such lands in order to take part in the carbon markets.

Forests: trade and climate links

Trade policy and trade agreements have powerful impacts on forests and forestry trade. They can encourage or discourage supplies of forest products (Presteman 2000). It is argued that there has been a rapid increase in forestry trade as a result of the General Agreement on Tariffs and Trade (GATT)/WTO agreement that reduces average world tariffs on forest products. At the same time countries can use non-tariff barriers (NTBs) and export tariffs to slow down the exports of forestry products. This can be on environmental or competitiveness grounds. Beyond the WTO, free trade agreements such as the North American Free Trade Agreement (NAFTA) and ones in the Asia-Pacific Economic Cooperation (APEC) have also contributed to increasing trade in forest products. Increasing manufacturing by forest producers can also contribute to rising GHGs with devastating consequences for women's lives and livelihoods.

Box 2.6 Governmental approaches to institutionalise forest–gender linkages

Cambodia (2014): Inter-ministerial gender task force to inform ongoing policy-making on forest and climate.

Ghana (2015): Gender sub-working group to enhance REDD+ [reducing emissions from deforestation and forest degradation in developing countries] policy process. The outcome was the Gender and REDD+ Action Plan (2015).

Vietnam: Lam Dong Province to be a pioneer for integrating gender within a provincial action plan for REDD+. Now a model for other provinces to follow.

Outcomes of such institutional mechanisms: anchor gender in overall national governance and assist with monitoring gender responsiveness of the policies and programmes by:

- raising awareness of gender issues within government;
- commissioning studies and surveys to feed policy deliberations;
- training civil servants and introducing gender parameters into public policy.

Source: Eggerts and Gari (2017).

Box 2.7 Forests and trade

Wood and wood products are the main commercial products of forests. They include fuelwood and charcoal (particularly important in developing countries), industrial roundwood, sawnwood, wood-based panels, wood pulp, paper and paperboard, semi-manufactures, and wooden articles.

Non-wood forest products (NWFPs) include food items (such as honey, nuts, berries, mushrooms and leaf fodder for animals), construction materials (including rattan and palm leaves), medicinal plants, other health care and cosmetic products, and items of cultural and spiritual significance. These NWFPs are primarily consumed at the local or national level, although some 150 are traded internationally in significant quantities. These include cork, essential oils, forest nuts, gum arabic, rattan and plant and animal components of pharmaceutical products. Around 80 per cent of the populace in developing countries use NWFP [sic] to meet nutrition and health needs (FAO 1999a). Particularly for the poor in developing countries, NWFPs can be of crucial importance, both for the material needs of the family and as a means to generate a little income. This can be especially true for women in communities located near forests, sometimes providing their only source of cash inflow.

... forests offer other social services including recreational opportunities, habitat for indigenous peoples, protection of natural and cultural heritage, maintenance of forest-related cultural and spiritual knowledge and values, enhancement of agricultural production systems, and improvement of urban, semi-urban, and rural living conditions (FAO 1999b). Moreover, forests provide several environmental services which are important both locally and globally. These include the conservation of biological diversity, soil and water conservation, and carbon storage and sequestration for mitigation of global climate change.

Source: Twarog (1999).

2.6.4 Energy: trade, climate change and sustainable development – gender dimensions

Energy and development is now a much discussed topic. SDG7 is 'Ensure access to affordable, reliable and sustainable modern energy services for all'.[42] In a development context, energy is particularly related to electrification for household, industrial, agricultural and transport uses. The underlying narrative is focused on the transformation of the energy system in developing countries (as well as developed countries) from one that is dependent on fossil fuels to one in which low-carbon fuels are dominant. The emphasis is currently on shifting from the drivers of climate change to more efficient and less carbon-intensive sources of power. Hence, the emphasis is on clean and renewable energy sources: hydro, geothermal, solar, wind, biofuels etc. At the same time, it is recognised that there is a significant deficit in access to energy for millions of women, men and children, particularly in rural areas in many developed countries, and most particularly in Africa and Asia.

According to the World Bank SE4ALL database,[43] rural access to energy is very low in Niger and Mali, with the proportions of the rural population with access to energy at 4.7 per cent and 1.8 per cent, respectively. It is higher in Nigeria, at about 41.1 per cent of the rural population (World Bank 2019b). ECREE (2015) also noted that in Africa the proportion of the population accessing modern fuels, including electricity, liquid and gaseous fuels such as liquefied petroleum gas and kerosene, is very low, for example 5 per cent in The Gambia, 12 per cent in Ghana and 24 per cent in Nigeria. Given this lack of penetration of modern fuels, men and women are dependent on fuel wood and traditional biomass. This has contributed to a 'documented annual death toll of 173,396 people each year; roughly half of them children with the largest numbers recorded in Nigeria, Côte d'Ivoire followed at a distance by Burkina Faso, Niger and Ghana' (IEA 2014, cited by ECREE 2015, p. 30).

Energy and sustainable development

Energy, its uses and its sources contribute to sustainable development as well as to climate change, which can undermine sustainable development. Fossil fuel energy sources and the use of energy in the production of goods and services have been implicated in the rise of GHGs and hence global warming and as a causal factor behind extreme weather events and other issues of climate variability. But energy is what powers domestic production and the distribution of goods domestically as well as international trade. So securing access to modern energy services for the women and men currently unserved will significantly improve health, employment and access to education and thus contribute to the SDGs; it will also drive sustainable trade.

It is also the case that access to modern energy sources is a driver of sustainable access to energy and to sustainable development. Energy is critical for gender equality and women's empowerment in improving their lives, reducing time deficits, increasing wellbeing and improving their trade production and productivity-related performance. Men and women require clean energy for improving health, enhancing productivity and ensuring livelihoods. But there are also challenges for sustainable development with some forms of clean energy. For example, the biofuels industry uses arable crops such as sugar and vegetables (e.g. maize and coconut oil), which can have adverse impacts on food security, and its need for large-scale land use and fodder for energy crop production can put it in conflict with the needs of traditional small farmers.

Gender and sustainable energy

Energy, its uses and strategies for obtaining and using clean energy sources are important for gender equality. As noted by ECOWAS, socio-economic and socio-cultural dynamics interact to create distinct patterns of use and benefits (ECOWAS Centre for Renewable Energy and Energy Efficiency 2015). This gives rise to gender differences in access to, uses of and effects of energy sources and appliances in the home and the community. As modern energy services can transform agriculture sector food production (ploughing, irrigation, cultivation), processing (grinding, milling and drying) and business (cold chain, access to market, pricing knowledge and higher-value products), they can have a tremendous positive impact on women's employment, health, wellbeing and livelihoods.

In all countries, energy is also important for water purification, distribution and irrigation and for energy production. In Africa and Asia, where women predominate in the agricultural sector, transformative changes in the energy system will directly affect agro processes and electricity for lighting, heating and cooking. But it can also impact energy prices and food security through the impact on price changes for food and agricultural inputs (ECOWAS 2015).

There are multiple ways to demonstrate how transformative change in the energy system can support the empowerment of women. Those most discussed in the energy and gender literature are through access to and participation in the energy value chain. The emphasis of gender activists, policy-makers and practitioners is therefore centred on:

> empowering women to engage in energy services to achieve autonomy, authority and decision-making power at work and thereby accelerate progress on international climate change and sustainable energy goals;

promoting strategies that enable the inclusion of women at every stage of the design, implementation, delivery and monitoring of energy services that responds to the needs of women;

redirecting capital to gender-responsive and socially inclusive energy business to support faster delivery of sustainable access to energy;

changing public policy and the private sector to empower women to engage in energy service delivery;

gathering data and proposing metrics to support better understanding and benchmarking of policy uptake in government and business, and the impact on the empowerment of women.

Energy: trade and climate links

Sustainable energy is not only a goal of the SDGs; it is also a key parameter integrated into the Paris Agreement. Energy, which contributed about 34 per cent of global human-made GHGs in 2010, is important to the long-term goals of climate stabilisation, clean air and better access to water. Furthermore, the Paris Agreement recognises the importance of addressing energy poverty in the context of preventing catastrophic climate change.[44] So the two spheres, trade and climate, interlink around the objective of ensuring sustainable energy, although sustainable energy is not yet an explicit objective of the trade arena. (Some researchers argue that renewable energy is protected by trade-related measures and, more importantly, that trade is a key pathway for channelling the diffusion of clean energy technologies.)

Energy is increasingly important in trade. Issues such as subsidies for both fossil fuels and clean and renewable energies are being raised as bones of contention among trade parties.[45] There is also the issue of carbon-based regulation on the flow of goods and services facilitated by energy generation and expenditure. Increasingly, energy sources powering modern transport systems such as air and maritime shipping are being targeted because of their high-emission contributions to global warming. Though such approaches are designed to address climate change, nonetheless they pose threats to developing countries' exports. These countries' exports are exposed to various emerging restrictive trade barriers and local content rules. At the same time, it is projected that there may be increasing opportunities in the rise in GVCs in solar photovoltaics, wind and other renewable energy sources for men and women in developing countries.

Contextualising trade and climate change in the emerging energy governance debate: are there any gender equity implications?

Least developed countries (LDCs), small island developing states (SIDS) and small vulnerable economies are commonly extremely vulnerable to (exogenous or endogenous) changes in their resource endowments. They are also categorised as largely open trading environments, where trade in goods and natural resources dominate their export portfolios. Thus, even small changes in the trading environment may have a deleterious effect on trade volumes, and thus on the producers, consumers and employees reliant on the sector. As noted earlier, women entrepreneurs, employees and subsistence farmers are heavily reliant on particular sectors of developing economies, such as agriculture, forestry and fisheries; for this reason, a more detailed, gender-lensed assessment of the impact of the emerging energy governance framework is warranted.

This present study on the trade, climate change and gender interface discusses how the increasing interconnectedness of these two global dynamics has an impact on gender equity, particularly as transmitted through changes in the trading environment, driven through necessary climate mitigation and adaptation interventions. Changes in the trading environment may occur as a consequence of the (in)actions of governments through adaptation and mitigation policy responses to climate change; or indeed as a consequence of changes in global agendas or developed countries' responses to climate change, particularly seeking energy-efficiency standards, carbon labelling etc., with attendant impacts on trade flows.

The interface between trade and energy is rapidly expanding within the global geopolitical and trade landscape. Countries require ever-increasing engagement with each other now and in the near future to wrestle with the issues that arise as a consequence of climate change and depleting natural resources typically converted into energy. There is an undisputed rising trajectory in the world's population, which influences the global demand for energy. The International Energy Agency estimates that global energy requirements will expand by approximately one quarter by 2040, largely as a consequence of increasing energy demand in emerging markets (IEA, 2018); China and India are expected to account for up to 50 per cent of the growth in global energy demand up to 2040 (BP Energy Outlook, 2018). As developing, emerging economies seek sustainable development to provide productive employment for their citizens, the need for energy to drive industrial and domestic use will be unstoppable. Reasonably, only the pursuit of renewables and new, efficient energy innovations will support increased use of energy without the negative impact of global warming. As stated by the WTO Director-General in a speech in April 2013, 'energy is a critical enabler of human well-being' (WTO 2013). It is incumbent upon policy-makers to seek out opportunities to maximise the potential of global cooperation to achieve greater, sustainable access to energy. This is reflected in SDG7, 'Ensure access to affordable, reliable, sustainable and modern energy for all'. Globally, women subsistence farmers have a critical need for energy access, which is not currently being met, in order to make better use of extension services and mechanise or harness new technologies in cultivation and harvesting processes. The extent to which an emerging energy governance framework will account for specific needs such as these remains to be seen. Certainly, agricultural associations that satisfactorily reflect the specific needs of all their members, including women, will be in a good position to articulate challenges of subsidence, desertification, over-reliance on rain-fed resource, and lack of irrigation particularly in the context of global warming affecting agricultural yields.

The WTO could do with ramping up constructive discussions between members on these issues. Arriving at a consensus on these issues is imperative for the WTO to play its role in developing a global energy governance framework that takes into account the sometimes divergent needs of different groups: advanced or developing economies. However, in recent years there has been increased debate on whether or not changes are required to the WTO rulebook in order to facilitate international energy policy objectives and considerations. That remains to be seen. There appears to be a sufficient institutional framework available at the WTO to facilitate open discourse between members as required, in an attempt to build the necessary consensus on the WTO's future position in global energy governance. Without these open discussions, policy-makers in the energy sector are denied the expertise of trade experts to arrive at a mutually agreed perspective on how trade fits into the transformative energy/climate change picture. Alternatively, or complementarily, such discussions, linking energy and investment and not just trade, could also be part of the UNFCCC discussions, especially in the areas of response measures, dealing with economic diversification and just transition of the workforce. An important test of a holistic approach is the inclusion of the needs of major users of domestic energy, e.g. women, and the challenging market access issues that a significant proportion of innovators face, e.g. SMEs.

What is the relevance of existing WTO provisions with respect to trade in energy?

It is hard to imagine many areas that are more closely interlinked to trade than energy is. Without access to energy, goods and services cannot be produced, and neither can those goods, services or indeed people move across borders; therefore, the ramifications for a country's trade competitiveness are obvious. Clearly, in the absence of energy, international trade cannot take place. Trade is also essential for energy processing, and investment in particular, to take place. Transparent and predictable rules of trade are critical in achieving the development of energy sources and, equally importantly, the global community's energy ambitions, including cost-effective access and sustainability.

Nationally, policy-makers require support to develop new policy guidance on how to enhance access to different energy producers and technologies in a developing-country context. Success in this area would enable energy supply to expand and be traded more readily across borders. Thus, undersupply in one country can be countered by the surpluses available in other neighbouring countries; this should facilitate regional integration and industrialisation.

Presently, there are insufficient global disciplines to address the nexus between energy and trade. This is a paradox in the making, driven by the compartmentalised manner in which global policy issues are discussed. Now more than ever, integrated, holistic approaches to regulating these issues are required. Energy (with its intimate link to climate change) and trade are a perfect example of this. However, this holistic approach requires a paradigm shift, which may take some time to come to fruition. Understandably, further discourse is required, which takes into account the need to assuage the concerns of natural-resource-rich, energy-exporting and energy-importing countries that have historic sovereignty and strategic concerns and are wary of commitments to international disciplines. The WTO's long-standing principles of transparency, non-discrimination and openness provide a useful institutional approach to frame discussions of relevance to the energy sector.

Issues of concern for the energy sector are those trade-restrictive practices such as subsidies, monopsony practices of state-owned enterprises, transport restrictions, limitations on competing in government procurement markets and NTBs to entry, particularly for new energy innovations, which often come from SMEs. WTO disciplines are applicable for the majority of these issues and can be clearly engaged with and improved upon given the fast-paced change in the global energy policy landscape as it grapples with the long-term implications of climate change.

Developmental preferences can be flexibly considered through the GATT instrument, specifically through the use of policies, aside from trade, in the interest of protecting the environment, for example. These flexibilities or provisions should also be considered for trade in natural resources before they are processed to produce energy and indeed even in basic form during the extractive process.

Definitions affect disciplining processes in trade

Much of the emerging discourse on the ramifications of existing WTO provisions for trade in energy goods and services is based on two areas of consideration: trade in natural resources required to produce energy, i.e. trade in fuels; and trade in energy as an entity with unique utility, i.e. trade in electricity, usually between two neighbouring countries. The trade in energy across borders is empirically measured as not very large presently; however, it will probably increase in developing regions as large energy infrastructure projects come on stream, as key countries develop and regions push for greater integration (notably Africa's Continental Free Trade Area). Conversely, trade in oil, gas and coal, typically used to produce energy, is very large, showing no signs of abating in the medium term except for considerations of dwindling reserves of natural resources. These distinctions are crucial to note and understand because they are disciplined (regulated) differently at the WTO, although some rules are in common. Moreover, notably both forms of trade in energy have particular, and different, ramifications for gender equality and climate change. Many of these differential impacts are realised through local/domestic policy decisions and flows of investment once they are implemented and delivered, resulting in specific outcomes.

A specific challenge still being considered at the WTO is that definitions of terms are still under debate. For example, is energy a good or a service, or perhaps both in some instances? This has been a crucial debate, as the WTO disciplines goods and services differently. Trade in energy is not specifically mentioned in the WTO treaty or the rules of the previous GATT. The Doha negotiating round on goods and services considers some of these issues. It is worth being cognisant that some of these challenges on definitional terms came to the fore only as a direct consequence of energy-producing members negotiating their accession to the WTO. It is uncontroversial, and largely agreed, that WTO rules are applicable to trade in natural resources; however, challenges remain with regard to how current WTO disciplines can be applied to the unique processes of trade in energy goods and/or services, production and delivery.

Other agreements under WTO of significance for the management of energy goods and services are the Trade-Related Aspects of Intellectual Property Rights (TRIPS) Agreements and the General Agreement on Trade in Services (GATS), a treaty of the WTO that came into force on 1 January 1995. Rules under GATS are of particular relevance for energy-related services, and the MFN principle is of the greatest significance: all trading economies subject to the WTO are treated equally, with the exception that no member country is required to consider foreign service suppliers in its market. As in the case of GATT, GATS does contain some flexibilities, allowing exceptions and set-asides particularly as these relate to regional trade agreements (RTAs).

A major factor in the drive towards more efficient energy goods and services is the rate at which new innovations and technologies appear, as well as access to those technologies. This is central to the discourse around the suitability of energy technologies in terms of environmental impacts and lifecycle of the infrastructures required to support those technologies. With so many innovative new technologies driving energy efficiency, the effectiveness of the TRIPS Agreement and the protection it affords is paramount to the discourse on energy efficiency.

Fossil fuel subsidies and their relevance to trade in energy

To address the extreme consequences of climate change, greater energy efficiency and, particularly, clean energies will be crucial to move the world onto a sustainable energy pathway. Governments are becoming more aggressive in pursuing clean energy sources (geothermal, wind, solar etc.), creating incentive frameworks at the supply and purchase ends of energy value chains, as they push for clean sustainable energy. On many fronts such actions are justified, not only because of the climate change intersectionality with energy production and consumption, but also harnessing new, more efficient innovations in the sector can drive competitiveness, increase export diversification and create new jobs. Yet there is a need to recognise the risk of increased rent-seeking behaviour through the proliferation of subsidies in the renewable energy sector at a time when WTO members are struggling to agree on the reduction of subsidies in historic sectors such as agriculture. However, the fossil fuel subsidies discussion has tended to remain at the level of the G20; although there have been some attempts to raise the issue at the WTO, these have not gained much traction.[46] A better approach to combat these potentialities would be to engage on modalities arising out of trade-related aspects of measures to encourage clean energy; there is sufficient institutional scope to facilitate such discourse. Clearly the WTO rulebook does allow for the protection of the environment, through restrictive trade if such actions are justifiable and not merely as disguised protectionism.

How to cope with the reform of fossil fuel subsidies, at both the consumer and production ends, has largely escaped debate within the WTO framework. Yet the connection between subsidies, climate change and energy consumption has created a new and emerging characteristic of the debate. The omission of this issue from WTO deliberations may be characterised as a missed opportunity to open dialogue and delve deeper into how to discipline this tool, to control for unintended consequences of subsidies. This omission has become more apparent, given that focused attention on the challenges arising from environmentally harmful subsidies in the fisheries sector is an important part of the Doha Round discussions being undertaken by WTO members.

A number of WTO disciplines are relevant to trade in energy (dependent on whether it is defined as a service or a good). For those WTO members that negotiate rules on a bilateral or regional basis outside the WTO, they would have to deliberate on how to control for existing energy-focused provisions within WTO agreements when planning other energy-related allowances outside the WTO framework. That intersectionality will be important to make the two regimes work. A good example is how to account for general and specific rules on agriculture subsidies with reference to the new specific energy subsidy rules.

Subsidies aside, WTO members have yet to capitalise on some low-hanging fruit, such as the potentialities proffered by the first multilateral environment agreements, particularly the mandate to open up trade in environmental goods and services. A significant volume of these goods and services, such as equipment for biogas production, solar water heaters and solar panels, and hydropower turbines, directly influences the production of clean energy and energy efficiency. A World Bank study on trade and climate change revealed that the elimination of tariffs and NTBs to clean technologies could lead to a 14 per cent expansion in trade in these products. The reduction of trade barriers on environmental goods and services could potentially give WTO members greater scope to negotiate access at a reduced cost to a wider range of clean energy technologies. Accelerating these efforts would have long-term tangible benefits for the environment and broadly sustainable development.

What does this all mean for gender equity?

Some purist trade policy-makers may argue that gender considerations are at the margins of any discourse on trade. Climate specialists appear to be more pragmatic; perhaps it is more visually apparent where the ramifications of climate change have an impact on divergent groups. Yet forward-thinking policy-makers are beginning to note that it is inevitable that these issues are considered in concert. The more business interests are considered in policy-making processes when building a sustainable economic strategy that addresses climate change and trade negotiations, the better will be the understanding that the producers of environmental goods and services are central to achieving country objectives. In discussing a possible framework for the intersectionality of trade, climate change and gender, there is an opportunity to look at what areas need to be incentivised in the drive for economic sustainability.

2.6.5 Tourism, climate change and sustainable development: gender dimensions

In developing countries, where tourism is a dominant economically active sector, it is a service industry that is reliant on other sectors that are themselves vulnerable to climate change impacts: agriculture, water etc. Tourism also requires several services such as housekeeping and customer contact, and the informal tourism sector provides a wide range of services to tourists – washing clothes, petty trading, cooking and childcare – that are closely related to the traditional caregiving roles associated with women's gender roles, responsibilities and expectations (Wedderburn and Grant Cummings 2017, p. 24; Williams 2002, p. 7).[47] It is also because of the significant horizontal and vertical segregation of occupations that gender-related inequalities are common in the sector (ILO cited in Wedderburn and Grant Cummings, 2017).

In many Caribbean countries, women are often over-represented in lower skills and lower paid areas, notably housekeeping and customer contact areas, with low-skilled and unskilled women often holding the most vulnerable jobs. They are under-represented in skilled kitchen work and in areas such as engineering and security as well as in terms of access to senior technical and managerial roles. (Wedderburn and Grant Cummings 2017, p.5)

Tourism is intimately connected to the sustainable development agenda, in which it features prominently in goals 8, 12 and 14. These goals focus on promoting 'sustained, inclusive and sustainable economic growth, full and productive employment and decent work for all'.[48] Tourism is one of the driving forces of global economic growth, and currently accounts for one in 11 jobs worldwide (UNWTO n.d.). According to the World Tourism Organization, tourism gives access to decent work opportunities in the tourism sector, particularly for youth and women. This is particularly important for the men and women in the tourism sector in small island developing states, which rely on the blue economy – of oceans and marine ecosystems.

The distinctiveness of tourism in global trade is that it 'moves people to the product rather than transporting the product of the people' (Pera and McLaren 1999). Tourism is also linked to other areas of the economy: agriculture, land and labour. It is inextricably intertwined with air transport, the major means used by tourists arriving in the South (a US$414 trillion industry), and communication. Given this, the liberalisation of tourism has major implications for social development and gender equality. Liberalisation tends to 'prioritize global commerce over everything: self-reliance of communities, human rights and health and safety' (Pera and McLaren 1999). Yoder (1998) writes that there is already a problem in enforcing standards in the tourism industry, such as prior informed consent, support for local initiatives and environmental regulations. Many of these prosocial and human development measures are already in conflict with WTO rules. As noted by Wallach and Sforza, WTO-orchestrated uniform global standards, which are designed by transnational corporations to promote harmonisation of standards, may 'facilitate the growth of consumer culture, [but they] militate against standards which reflect differences in cultural values. Such differences are seen as undesirable because they fragment the global market' (Wallach and Sforza 1999).

Trade rules such as the so-called Singapore issues in the WTO (investment, competition policy and government procurement) may limit opportunities to create sustainable tourism alternatives and may put the brakes on the continued development of 'pro-poor'-oriented approaches to tourism. In addition, investment and competition rules may affect indigenous and local control over tourism products. This is because it will limit countries' ability to put conditions on types of investment they receive. It will rather grant more rights to foreign investment and will increase the leakage of profits out of a host country. Competition policy will affect the rights of communities to regulate which companies can set up business in their land. The Agreement on Trade-Related Investment Measures (TRIMS) already restricts countries' rights to require companies to purchase local materials, and the MFN provision makes it illegal for countries to reward companies that hire locally or have good environmental practices. (Yoder 1999; Pera and McLaren 1999; Pleumarom 1999). Furthermore, it is not clear what the impacts and implications of issues such as trade facilitation and e-commerce are likely to mean for women's empowerment and gender equality. GATS impacts tourism via rules and regulations on the production, distribution and marketing of tourism services (mode of supply); tour operators that supply services across borders with other countries (cross-border supply); international visitors (consumption abroad); the flow of international hotel chains, branches or full ownership of hotel chains and agencies in other countries (commercial presence); and the activities of tour guides and hotel managers (presence of natural persons).

Domestic regulations rules, which are currently under negotiation in the WTO, may affect governments' use of taxation policies to prevent de-industrialisation and de-agriculturalisation, while with liberalisation governments may not be able to impose commodity taxes to improve the welfare effects of tourism. Governments may not be able to mitigate or limit the impact of the outflow of repatriated earnings from foreign direct investment, which will result in reduced welfare.

GATS may also prove a problem for eco- and heritage tourism development. Eco-tourism does not have substantial start-up costs and can provide more sustainable jobs, preserve and conserve the resource base, and help to ensure that more tourist dollars remain in the country. These benefits tend to accrue more when there is planning and management with a long-term perspective and with local community participation, which may be greatly constrained under the rules of GATS.

Thus, without complementary flanking measures, GATS could ultimately have serious implication for pro-poor tourism that attempts to generate net benefits to the poor. The core of this strategy is to 'unlock opportunities for the poor with tourism rather than to expand the overall size of the sectors, to spread income beyond the individual earners to the wider community, and to address the negative social and environmental impacts' (Pera and McLaren 1999). However, this requires domestic regulations to remove some barriers to entry at local levels and for local entrepreneurs, as well as to protect countries' ability to participate effectively in tourism.

Notes

1 There are no internationally agreed-upon definitions of these approaches, and many countries and researchers use them in different ways. However, in general, green growth refers to fostering 'economic growth and development' (including a stable climate) 'while ensuring that natural assets continue to provide the resources and environmental services on which our well-being relies' (OECD 2012, p. 8).
2 In the same vein, in seeking to effectively reduce carbon dioxide emissions while maintaining economic growth, different countries have begun to implement what are known collectively as low-emission development strategies (also known as low-carbon development strategies) in terms of

'forward-looking national economic development plans or strategies that encompass low-emission and/or climate-resilient economic growth'. See Yuan et al. (2011) and World Bank (2012).
3 Chatham House and Vivid Economics (2010), *Evidence for Action: Gender Equality and Economic Growth*, available at: http://www.oecd.org/dac/gender-development/45568595.pdf. [accessed 6 August 2019].
4 Members, such as the European Union, have hence committed to having a trade and sustainable development chapter in some of their free trade agreements (e.g. EU agreements with South Korea, Central America, Colombia, Georgia, Moldova and the Ukraine). These chapters purport to promote 'sustainable management of natural resources in areas of low carbon development, forestry, fisheries, biodiversity, fight illegal harvesting practices and promote corporate social responsibility and fair and ethical initiatives. http://ec.europa.eu/trade/policy/policy-making/sustainable-development/ [accessed 2 August 2019]. As of 2015 and the coming into force of the Paris Agreement (the UNFCCC), the EU has announced that it will make agreements with only countries that signed up to the Paris Agreement. https://www.independent.co.uk/news/world/europe/eu-trade-deal-paris-climate-change-accord-agreement-cecilia-malmstr-m-a8206806.html [accessed 2 August 2019].
5 Subsequent meetings and complementary arenas both at and following Rio also continued this trend. For example, Agenda 21 highlighted the importance of promoting an open, non-discriminatory and equitable MTS, as did the 2002 Johannesburg plan of implementation.
6 UNCTAD. (2015) The role of international trade in the post-2015 development agenda. P3, para 6 https://unctad.org/meetings/en/SessionalDocuments/cid33_en.pdf
7 Informal trading accounts for a significant portion of the exports of many low-income countries, e.g. Uganda (86 per cent of official export flow, 2006) and Benin (ten times the official export).
8 **Food justice:** includes women's independent access to and control over land; an end to land grabs and land dispossessions of an involuntary and/or coercive nature; seeds being banked, shared amongst and controlled by women and other small-scale farmers; the implementation of laws, policies and government programmes that support an agro-ecological small-scale family-based model of agricultural production. Food security does not adequately describe this.
9 Research on Brazil (Gaddis and Pieters 2017) shows mixed outcomes, while a preliminary report on Indonesia (Kis-Katos and Sparrow 2015) argues that rates are higher for men than for women.
10 UNCTAD's trade, gender and development programme, among other activities, has systematically produced multiple series of case studies on trade and gender (at least seven to date), runs a regular seven-week e-learning course on trade and gender, offers a trade and gender toolbox, builds national capacity on trade and gender issues, and has organised at least one yearly meeting on the topic between 2016–2019.
11 Much of this will depend on whether or not e-commerce is to be treated better than or at the same level as offline (now often described as bricks and mortar) commerce; if treated e commerce is treated the same as bricks and mortar commerce, then it may potentially reduce some opportunities usually identified with ecommerce, such as reduced transaction costs of trade, lowering the cost of participation for new entrants into commerce/trade.
12 It is not yet a reality. It is centred around the existing ASEAN agreements, and the main new trade relationship within the Regional Comprehensive Economic Partnership is between India and China.
13 Thus far it has received 22 ratifications, out of 54 countries (or 55 if the Sahrawi are added).
14 There is currently a proposal on MSMEs in the WTO, including for a work programme on small and medium-sized enterprises (SMEs). It was proposed by the Philippines in 2015 after the Asia-Pacific Economic Cooperation (APEC) trade ministers' meeting in Boracay called for action to globalise MSMEs. 'We reaffirm our commitment to implement the Boracay Action Agenda to Globalize MSMEs through initiatives that strengthen MSMEs' competitiveness and ability to participate in Global Value Chains (GVCs) and look forward to the stocktake and 2018 mid-term review by November. We support efforts to improve the capacity of MSMEs to operate in an environmentally conscious manner through the APEC Strategy for Green Sustainable and Innovative MSMEs' (APEC 2018).
15 Export subsidies are possible for enterprises in LDCs and other 'Annex VII' countries with low income per capita.
16 Work on MSME in the context of trade was first mooted in APEC, but seems to be tapering off at the multilateral level.

17 Water justice refers to the access of individuals to clean water https://en.wikipedia.org/wiki/Water_politics#Water_justice The Water Justice Project run by the Transnational Institute is part of a global movement to reclaim public water and supports, public, effective, participatory public water services.' https://www.tni.org/en/page/about-water-justice-project

18 Women may also be differentially impacted upon by the design and development of physical infrastructure, such as roads and ports that would be part of the dynamics of any trade-related infrastructure under Aid for Trade [AfT]. The focus on what kinds of infrastructure will receive priority attention and support--whether it is feeder roads or simply main roads are critical to the survival and expansion of women and small farmers in ensuring access to market and their ability to be independent of middlemen; it may also lessen their dependency on lesser remunerative farm-gate pricing structure

19 The AfDB et al states that the adverse impacts of climate change on poverty 'will be most striking in the developing nations because of their dependence on natural resources, and their limited capacity to adapt to a changing climate. Within these countries, the poorest, who have the least resources and the least capacity to adapt, are the most vulnerable' (African Development Bank et al. 2003, cited by IPCC 2007).

20 Data for the Pacific are from Aucan (2018). Because of its near proximity to the equator, sea level rise (SLR) will be more pronounced in the Caribbean (Nurse et al. 2014). Some forecasts predict SLR up to 1 or 2 metres over the 21st century if the global average temperature rises by 2-2.5°C (Nurse et al. 2014; Simpson et al. 2010). Furthermore, the impact on 'impacts of SLR would not be uniform among the CARICOM [Caribbean Community] nations, with some projected to experience severe impacts from even a 1m SLR' due to 'the geophysical characteristics of the islands and their different coastal topographic settings, which also give rise to different vulnerability to climate change and SLR (for example, coastal plains below 10 m, low lying island (Guyana, Belize and Suriname, volcanic island coasts (the Bahamas, Barbuda and the Grenadines) volcanic island coasts (Dominica, Grenada, St Kitts & Nevis, St Lucia, St Vincent and Montserrat), and 'varied geophysical characteristics, Antigua, the Bahamas, Haiti, Jamaica and Trinidad and Tobago' (Simpson et al. 2010).

21 Changes in temperature and rainfall will alter the geographical ranges of vector-borne diseases such as malaria and dengue fever. Women, particularly pregnant women, and children are susceptible to these diseases. Malaria is linked to perinatal mortality, low birthweight and maternal anaemia (OECD et al. 2003).

22 There is some reversal of the downward trend in child or forced marriages. That has been argued to be due to conflict and increasingly to climate change and consequent adaptation strategies as well as the interlinkage between climate change and conflicts (Chamberlain 2017, Care 2016; Alston et al., 2014).

23 NAMAs were established in 2007 at UNFCCC Conference of the Parties (COP) 135 as an element of the Bali Action Plan (Decision 1/CP.13), and implementation began after 2009.

24 The NAMA leveraged the newly issued net metering regulations, which allowed electricity customers who generate their own electricity from solar and wind power to feed the electricity they do not use back into the grid (CCAP n.d.).

25 This is primarily because, as noted by the report, releasing information on NAMAs is voluntary and at the discretion of governments and project sponsors, so these databases rarely include comprehensive NAMA design documents. Without access to this key information for the purpose of a gender assessment, it is difficult to conduct a statistical analysis of how gender has been integrated into NAMAs to date.

26 Bangladesh has made an unconditional commitment to reduce emissions by 5 per cent below business as usual by 2030, Jamaica by 7.8 per cent and Namibia by 8.9 per cent. In the 20-30 per cent range are Tanzania (10-20 %), Nigeria (20 %), Uganda (22 %), St Lucia (23 %) and St Vincent and the Grenadines (22 %). In the 30–40 per cent range are India (33–35 %), Malaysia, St Kitts and Nevis (35 % each) and Ghana (45 %). Above 50 per cent are Tuvalu (50 %) and 81 per cent (from 2006 level). Countries such as Tonga and Nepal express their reduction commitments in terms of improved energy efficiency and decrease in total energy consumption (Tonga) and decrease in fossil fuel dependency (Nepal, 50 %).

27 It is predicted that by 2100 in sub-Saharan Africa there is likely to be a 2–7 per cent loss of GDP due to losses in agriculture, and a 0.4–1.3 per cent loss in Central Africa. It is important to note that agriculture is a major part of African countries' NDCs.
28 Climate-change-induced warming can lead to wider transmission of malaria; 'rising temperature extends the habitats of the mosquitoes that carry the malaria parasite, shifting the boundaries of latitude and altitude for malaria transmission – for example, many highland areas in Burundi, Kenya and Uganda that have historically been classed as malaria-free are now experiencing epidemics' (Sulaiman 2007). Floods and higher rainfalls are associated with new breeding grounds for mosquitoes in Mozambique, and droughts in sub-Saharan Africa lead to declining water levels and rising stagnant pools of water (Sulaiman and Suad 2007).
29 For example, in the Democratic Republic of the Congo fewer than 10 per cent of women are landowners, only 2 per cent of women have access to credit from financial institutions and, because of this, 42 per cent of women take loans from family and friends at exorbitant interest rates. Women of the Democratic Republic of the Congo also lack access to markets. In Côte d'Ivoire, according to the National Institute of Statistics, women make up almost 70 per cent of the agricultural labour force, but only 3 per cent of women own the land that they cultivate (UN Women 2016).
30 This is generally so except in Senegal, where women are increasing earnings with the expansion of large-scale commerce in the agricultural sector (UN Women 2016).
31 CSA provides greater policy space for more holistic approaches to agriculture, it nonetheless operates within an apolitical framework that is narrowly focused on technical fixes at the level of production. This depoliticised approach to the global food system tends to validate existing policy agendas and minimise questions concerning power, inequality and access.
32 Agricultural business is variously defined; but the broader category includes agro-industry, including suppliers of inputs—seeds, fertilizers, fuel and credit; the agriculture sector broadly includes crop, livestock, fishery, aquaculture, forestry, and the distribution of food and non-food products from agriculture (Khalfani 2015). Agro-industry can also include post-harvest activities involving the transformation, preservation and preparation of agriculture products for intermediary or final consumption (Khalfani 2015). The agro-industry manufacturing subsector processes raw material and intermediate products derived from agriculture, fisheries, livestock and forestry. It also includes manufacturing of food, beverages, tobacco, textile and clothing, wood products, furniture, paper and paper products, and rubber production. It is a process of transforming agriculture produce into processed commodities for the market (p. 13) and also involves artisanal, minimally processed and packaged agricultural raw material, and industries and technology interface in the processing of intermediate goods and fabrication of final products derived from agriculture.
33 This is more concentrated in Latin America, which accounts for 43 per cent of developing countries.'
34 According to Waskey (2007), 'Non-traditional agricultural exports (NTAEs) are agricultural products that have not previously been consumed or planted as cash crops in a country. NTAEs include fruits, vegetables, flowers, nuts, and spices. NTAEs are growing in importance globally because of their economic value; they make up the overwhelming majority of trade taking place in the horticultural and floricultural sectors of both producer and consumer countries.'
35 Fisheries can also be discussed in terms of place – inland (river and lake), sea/marine – as well as in terms of type (e.g. capture or aquaculture). Currently, fisheries subsidies negotiations in principle target only marine capture fisheries.
36 Fish represent 58 per cent of total animal protein consumption and a key source of vitamins and minerals in Bangladesh.
37 The FAO International Plan of Action on IUU is a globally agreed framework but is not legally binding.
38 There has been a series of case studies and articles documenting the situation of women in fisheries in Africa, in particular in the Sahel region. See, for example, COMFISH (Collaborative Management for a Sustainable Fisheries Future), a project funded by the United States Agency for International Development (Benavides 2018a,b; Coastal Resources Center n.d.; World Bank 2019a).
39 According to WorldFish Center, though it is often considered that women are less involved in fisheries activities in countries such as Bangladesh, in reality women are heavily involved in fish production systems: feed preparation, fertilisation of ponds, feeding shrimps etc., as well as

post-harvest activities and aquaculture. In addition, research points out that post-harvest activities provide a range of direct livelihood opportunities for poor women. This will disappear if fish production decreases, and with it women's access to income and food – including access to essential vitamins and minerals in the diet of women, who tend to give food priority to their husbands and children (WorldFish Center, Bangladesh). https://www.worldfishcenter.org/news-updates

40 The intertidal zone is the area that is above water at low tide and underwater at high tide (in other words, the area between tide marks). These areas are often home to many species of crabs, shellfish, shallow water fish and many other animals. Many environmental things affect these areas, for example, waves, sunlight, salinity, wind, and water tide (Wikipedia).

41 There are a number of institutional reports, academic assessments and newspaper reports on the conditions of women in the fish sector in Senegal and the Sahel region in general. These include Kwan (2017), Benavides (2018a,b); Beatley and Edwards (2018a), Beatley (2018), Coastal Resources Center (n.d.) and World Bank (2019a) and COMFISH (Collaborative Management for a Sustainable Fisheries Future), a project funded by the United States Agency for International Development, https://www.pri.org/stories/2018-03-30/senegalese-women-turn-exporting-fish-spite-local-shortages (accessed 6 August 2019).

42 Globally, 1 billion men and women have no access to electricity and 2.9 billion use solid fuels (wood, coal, dung) for cooking and heating.

43 SE4ALL Global Tracking Framework. https://www.worldbank.org/en/topic/energy/publication/Global-Tracking-Framework-Report

44 This is important because two out of every five persons on Earth have no access to clean fuel; 2.5 million cook with polluting fuels and face premature deaths.

45 There are at least 40 antidumping and countervailing duty cases on renewable energy (biofuels, solar and wind) in dispute through the various trade compliance and dispute settlement mechanisms.

46 See, for example, New Zealand's ministerial statement of December 2017 encouraging the WTO to address 'the global harm being caused by inefficient fossil fuel subsidies' (New Zealand 2019). The G20 language has an important caveat: the effects on the poor are to be minimised. The OECD is coordinating G20 voluntary peer reviews of fossil fuel subsidies, but it is not clear if gender is integrated into these reviews. (OECD 2019).

47 This may vary geographically and according to gender norms in some settings, but it is the norm for areas such as the Caribbean. (For more in-depth treatment of this theme across the Commonwealth, see Williams 2003; Equations 2000, 2001). Wedderburn et al., 2017,also notes that women are 'under-represented in skilled kitchen work and in areas such as engineering and security as well as in terms of access to senior technical and managerial roles.'

48 The sector's contribution to job creation is recognised in target 8.9: 'By 2030, devise and implement policies to promote sustainable tourism that creates jobs and promotes local culture and products' (UNWTO n.d.). With regard to SDG12, 'Ensure sustainable consumption and production patterns', the tourism sector can adopt sustainable consumption and production practices and so can play a significant role in accelerating the global shift towards sustainability (UNWTO). This is recognised in target 12.b, 'Develop and implement tools to monitor sustainable development impacts for sustainable tourism that creates jobs and promotes local culture and products'. Please see, for example, the Sustainable Tourism Programme of the 10-Year Framework of Programmes on Sustainable Consumption and Production Patterns.

Chapter 3

Gender Issues in Trade and Climate Change Governance

3.1 Gender and governance issues within the trade debate[1]

Gender issues and women's empowerment concerns are central to and inextricably intertwined with issues of the pathways of trade expansion and trade intensification on decent work, wages, including gender wage gaps, and the potential of female- (and male-) owned micro- and small businesses to scale up to increasingly large enterprises that would enable sustainable livelihoods, decent working conditions and a life with dignity. These issues have been the persistent concerns of gender and women's rights activists, academic researchers and policy-makers working on international trade and development from a feminist perspective.

Undeniably, trade agreements and trade policy can provide support for some of the critical dimensions of empowerment such as decent working conditions, sustainable employment, income and wages, markets and opportunity for the profitable growth of MSMEs and farmers. These policy frameworks can also enhance the environment for the provision of social and other services, reinforcing governmental revenues through the collection of trade taxes and other related sources, arising from trade expansion.

The Commonwealth Secretariat, with funding from the UK Department for International Development, implemented a two-year (2005–2007), comprehensive training and capacity-building programme focused on gender, trade and export promotion across the regions of the Commonwealth. UNCTAD's work, and numerous other case studies and analyses, present a stylised picture of trade and gender. Some of the key issues are highlighted below:

- Trade liberalisation does not create structural gender inequalities, but may create conditions that can either enhance women's economic situation or exacerbate pre-existing gender inequalities and biases.

- The trade reform that accompanies trade liberalisation at the domestic level can affect – for better or worse – conditions in the labour market, relative prices for products, and resources and government revenues. It may, hence, adversely affect government expenditures on a variety of measures that are important for social development broadly, and women's empowerment more specifically.

- The distributional effects of trade policies (through price and wage channels) are gender differentiated.

- Trade policies can and do have negative impacts on both paid and unpaid work, which, considering that women are the majority of workers in trade sectors, can worsen women's status, unless gender issues are taken into consideration by policy-makers and/or efforts are made to assist women and men to overcome the negative effects through the implementation of complementary support measures.

- Women and men have differential access to export promotion strategies and programmes, and this also affects the success of such strategies.

- Challenges faced by women in reaching the export market are more than twice as severe as those in the domestic market (Tandon 2003): stringent quality standards, stricter conditions – time and quantities of supplies – and complex logistics of exporting may present barriers to entry in export markets that may prevent women, more than men, from taking advantage of new economic opportunities.

- Absorption into global production systems (voluntary or not, in terms of participation, the nature of the intervention in GVCs and the share of control over resources) may not automatically benefit women or micro and small enterprises in general. Proactive policies need to be in place to generate sustained benefits.

- Trade facilitation measures, likewise, may not automatically benefit women and other small producers, especially if such measures are simply geared to facilitate transnational companies, and if such measures adversely affect government revenue and expenditure allocations to the disadvantage of MSMEs.[2]

Drawing on the work of Carr and Williams (2010), as well as UNCTAD's multi-country case studies (2014, 2015 and 2016) and the expert group discussion on the topic of trade, gender equality and women's empowerment convened by UNCTAD in May 2016, the most accurate answer about the empowerment effect of trade on women is that it depends on the following:

- The extent to which trade itself promotes development and does not simply extract resources and perpetuate dependence on cheap labour.

- The extent to which trade policy and trade agreements goes beyond the emphasis on simplistic notions of trade expansion and intensification, and policy-makers and practitioners pay sufficient attention to wages, the nature and conditions of the expected job creation and the implication for women's empowerment. Trade expansion on its own does not generate sustained improvement in women's overall situation, though there may be marginal and temporary improvements in some women's economic and social status, through employment gains.

- The extent to which trade policies, trade regulation and trade development projects and programmes determined by national governments are in synergy with the implementation of other policies, local, national and international, with implications for who benefits and who loses. These include commitments and policies around human rights, labour conditions, gender equality and now climate change.

Furthermore, Dunn et al. (2010), in examining trade policies and trade agreements such as the economic partnership agreements (EPAs) in the Caribbean, argue that gender-responsive interventions should include supporting the full enforcement of core labour standards and antidiscrimination legislation; promoting institutional mechanisms that foster small female producers and traders' participation; designing agricultural vocational training and extension services to meet the specific needs of female farmers; promoting gender audits of trade-related administrative procedures; financing physical infrastructural projects that reduce women's time and energy burdens; protecting women's rights over their own financial assets and assisting them in claiming a fair remuneration for contributing their labour to family business; and measures to contribute to enhance men's and women's agricultural productivity, including facilitating access of female small farmers to capital, knowledge and capacity to invest in the adoption of new technologies.

Other researchers support the above interventions and additionally point to the importance of broader measures that are linked to the degree and scope of developing countries' policy space for economic policy initiatives, including financial policies (such as guaranteed loans schemes or micro-finance plus), and support for business development activities that target both male and female enterprises equitably. Measures also need to be taken to avoid tariff cuts, which have a regressive impact, such as improving the consumption of well-off households while making goods and services consumed by vulnerable groups less affordable. Ultimately, there must be unqualified support for the unpaid work, and other social safety-net work, provided by women and men in communities.

As noted in Chapter 2 of this report, women in most developing countries work in sectors, such as agriculture, textiles and clothing, that are not only very important for export performance but also vulnerable to the effects of trade liberalisation. Yet, as pointed out above, the statistics (numbers of women in trade) remain dismal. If this were simply an accounting exercise, it would not be a serious policy issue. But it is not. Increasingly, research is showing that the under-recognition of women's activities leads to low concentration of economic resources to support productivity growth, and lack of progress in widening and deepening their contributions to trade has serious economic costs. Women produce 50 per cent of global good products and constitute on average 43 per cent of the agricultural labour force in developing countries (FAO 2011).[3] In some countries, they are more than 70 per cent of the non-agricultural informal employees. Women are also roughly 90 per cent of the workforce in EPZs (e.g. in Honduras, Jamaica and Sri Lanka). But in most countries women still earn on average 60–70 per cent as much as men (World Bank 2015b); even in sectors where women may have better pay and more stable jobs, such as in the EPZ sector (World Bank and the WTO 2015).[4] Furthermore, it is reported that, although 40 per cent of SMEs worldwide are women-owned business, only 15 per cent of exporting firms are led by women (International Trade Centre 2017). Much of this could be caused by discriminatory practices against women. Women-owned SMEs are reported to face higher export costs, delay in processing export permits, lack of access to trade finance and exclusion from distribution networks. In 2016, research found that 90 per cent of 173 countries had at least one law impeding women's economic opportunities (World Bank 2016a). The economic costs of these discriminations are growing. For example, economic and social discrimination against women costs the continent about US$105 billion a year or 6 per cent of its GDP (African Human Development Report, 2016). The World Bank's *Doing Business Report* argues that globally the elimination of all forms of discrimination against women would increase per capita productivity by 40 per cent (World Bank 2016b).[5] To cap this off, one must highlight the robustness of findings across the developing world that women invest most of their income (some argue as much as 90 %) back into their families and communities. Women make financial investments in education and health, and physically invest in unpaid household and community work. All of this, researchers argue, has a snowball effect on society that leads to increasing living standards and poverty reduction.

These and other factors have led to a growing focus on the relationship between trade and gender, and the emergence of gender and trade programmes and projects. Concerns and actions about women's roles in, contribution to, and benefit from trade intensification and expansion are reaching a critical turning point in terms of their acceptance in discussions about trade policy, trade regulation, and trade and development. However, there has not been significant uptake of integrating these concerns within the overarching content of trade negotiations and agreements, in which most issues are couched in gender-neutral terms: 'people', 'farmers', target groups or beneficiaries. These are easy formulations for presumed gender-neutral and gender-blind treatment in development and trade issues. Firstly, trade expansion and liberalisation leads to changes in the structure of production, with sectors producing for export likely to expand and other sectors sensitive to import competition likely to contract. This, in turn, causes changes in the level and distribution of employment of different categories of workers employed with different intensities by different sectors. The economic volatility often associated with production for world markets is also likely to affect the quality and security of employment differently for various groups of workers and producers, with small-scale producers and low-skill workers more often bearing the brunt. Gendered employment effects from greater trade openness are to be expected because of the different distribution of women and men across tradable and non-tradable sectors, combined with limited substitutability between female and male labour due to rigid gender roles in the labour market.

Additionally, trade liberalisation affects men's and women's time allocation, and women's bargaining power and access to and control of resources such as land and income. At the same time, because of gender-specific discrimination and biases that negatively affect women's access to productive assets, new technology may also act as a barrier to increasing economies of scale by women-owned enterprises; thus, women are often more constrained than men in reaping the benefits of trade expansion (Korinek 2005).

Increasingly, initial concerns about gender being a 'new' issue or a potential source of conditionality are easing as more governments are realising the importance taking the initiative in addressing gender in trade. The reasons for this are two-fold. First, they recognise that gender equality is a commitment emanating from instruments (the Convention on the Elimination of all Forms of Discrimination Against Women (CEDAW), the Beijing Platform for Action and various regional initiatives) that those governments have signed and implemented in many national initiatives. Most governments are also explicitly committed to the social equity and social development objectives of the SDGs to be achieved by 2030.

Second, growing empirical evidence on trade and gender show the importance of addressing the gender constraints and challenges for successful export expansion and the improvement of trade competitiveness. As a result of work on value-chain analysis on mango exports (Kenya and Mali), the garment sector (Lao PDR) and women's small businesses (South Sudan), many governments are taking actions to mitigate the negative effects of the constraints arising from technological disparities, factor market rigidity, information bias and the intersectoral mobility of resources on women's productivity, livelihood and overall empowerment (Baba Steve Fickr 2012; ECOWAS and ITC (n.d.); Sangho et al., 2010).

Commonwealth countries' activities have focused on generating good practices that promote greater benefits from trade, gender equality and women's empowerment. Uganda has gender-sensitised its national export strategy (see case study in subsection 3.1.2). In 2009, the position of the foreign trade policy (FTP) in India was that the linkages of trade and gender issues had been established; thereafter, in collaboration with the Commonwealth Secretariat, the Ministry of Commerce constituted a steering committee involving policy-makers, academia and civil society; subsequently a national seminar was organised and further research and capacity-building on the gender and trade dimension were undertaken. For example, studies were commissioned consisting of data analysis of Gender Profile in Export Oriented Industries in India (GATI); and the design of Gender Sensitive Foreign Trade Policy for India (IIFT & CUTS), Identification of gender sensitive products at 6-digit HS (RIS), Engendering India's FTP (CWS)[6] (Ratna 2010a).

According to Ratna (2010a), the government of India conducted a study on gender and trade in 2009 and explored an approach to a gender-based FTP. Ratna raises the issue that governments such as India's can have a defensive position in seeking to protect the gender-sensitive products/sectors (sectors that employ high percentages of women) from commitments to liberalisation in the WTO and RTAs and/or an offensive position that seeks market access for such products/sectors. He further queries if there can be positive discrimination in FTPs. Though positive discrimination may not appear relevant to FTP, incentives are more focused towards sectors in which there is a strong presence of a female workforce.[7]

3.1.1 Institutional approaches to integrating gender and trade

Among Commonwealth countries that are lead advocates of FTAs that include gender issues directly or indirectly, Canada and Australia take the approach of including reference to broad social and labour rights issues in their trade agreements. But few Commonwealth countries originating FTAs go as far as some countries in Latin America, which include direct reference to gender and, in at least two cases, address gender equality issues in specific chapters. The FTA between Chile and Uruguay (2016) and the updated Canada–Chile FTA (2017) include stand-alone chapters on trade and gender. In the Chile–Uruguay FTA, which is the first trade agreement to include gender, gender has a stand-alone chapter, Chapter 15. Both of these agreements include provisions that consider broad gender equality areas that benefit women (in terms of skills, capacity-building, leadership and decision-making), and trade and gender committees as a mechanism to operationalise the gender chapters.[8] Other FTAs in the Latin American region target gender issues for selective treatment, for example the agreement between Central America and the Dominican Republic (Chapter 16, Annex 16.5m 3(l)), the Canada–Chile Agreement on Labour Cooperation (Article 11: Cooperative Activities, 1(m)) and the NAFTA Agreement on Labour Cooperation (Annex 1 on labour principles, paragraphs 7 and 8).

Some researchers argue that the language in these agreement is mostly hortatory and not legally binding and point out that specific gender-related standards that could affect trade agreements such as equal pay for equal work are not included ... [rather] reference is made to the implementation of gender equality commitments of global conventions (i.e., CEDAW and the SDGs) (Frohmann 2017; Zarilli 2017). There are no specific goals, nor do dispute settlement mechanisms apply to these chapters and provisions in any of these agreements. More importantly, the provisions/chapters do not address in a direct way the potential impact of trade liberalisation on women's wellbeing and economic empowerment. Nonetheless, the Chile–Uruguay agreement is still considered the gold standard with respect to integrating gender into trade agreements.

Several regional trade agreements and free trade agreements in the global economy make direct and indirect references to gender issues. The Caribbean Community's (CARICOM's) Article 17 is one of the few regional agreements among Commonwealth countries that indirectly reference gender as part of the broad approach that links social and labour (Box 3.1). In addition, the Caribbean Forum (CARIFORUM) 2008 EPA with the EU (the successor to the Cotonou Agreement[9]) maintains the gender commitments from Cotonou but does not elaborate on them (Frohmann 2017). As noted by Jackson and Wedderburn (2009), women are mentioned but not elaborated upon in the context of the broader objectives of sustainable development (see also Frohmann 2017). This is in contrast to other RTAs such as the Andean Community's Cartagena Protocol Article 130 and its Sucre Protocol Article 24.

However, it must be highlighted that regional economic institutions in Africa would seem to have gone the farthest in integrating gender and trade into their policy and operational frameworks; they have undertaken the most comprehensive approach to gendering trade policy and agreements. All four major regional institutions – the Common Market for Eastern and Southern Africa (COMESA), the East African Community (EAC), the Economic Community of West African States (ECOWAS) and the Southern African Development Community (SADC) – have well-established frameworks for the integration and promotion of gender equality and the empowerment of women. Recently, there has been an increased commitment to include a specific focus on gender and trade.

> **SADC:** Gender is a central aim of its policy and operation framework. It is noted for having a holistic approach to the issues. It has had a Gender and Development Protocol since 2008 and has implemented gender mainstreaming over the same period. However, there is no clear time frame for mainstreaming a gender perspective.

> **Box 3.1 Gender in Cotonou and references to social issues in CARICOM**
>
> **CARICOM Revised Treaty of Chaguaramas – Article 17**
>
> The Council for Human and Social Development
>
> 2. Subject to the provisions of Article 12, COHSOD shall be responsible for the promotion of human and social development in the Community. In particular, COHSOD shall:
>
> …
>
> (d) establish policies and programmes to promote the development of youth and women in the Community with a view to encouraging and enhancing their participation in social, cultural, political and economic activities;
>
> **Cotonou Agreement – Article 31 – Gender issues**
>
> Cooperation shall help strengthen policies and programmes that improve, ensure and broaden the equal participation of men and women in all spheres of political, economic, social and cultural life. Cooperation shall help improve the access of women to all resources required for the full exercise of their fundamental rights. More specifically, cooperation shall create the appropriate framework to:
>
> a. integrate a gender-sensitive approach and concerns at every level of development cooperation including macroeconomic policies, strategies and operations; and
>
> b. encourage the adoption of specific positive measures in favour of women such as:
>
>   i. participation in national and local politics;
>
>   ii. support for women's organisations;
>
>   iii. access to basic social services, especially to education and training, health care and family planning;
>
>   iv. access to productive resources, especially to land and credit and to labour market; and
>
>   v. taking specific account of women in emergency aid and rehabilitation operations.
>
> Source: Coche et al. (2006).

COMESA: Articles 154 and 155 of the treaty recognise the importance of ensuring the effective and equal participation of women and men. COMESA has adopted a regional gender policy. Gender mainstreaming is under implementation. Its gender policy has a comprehensive gender and development strategy to reduce gender inequality and advance gender-responsive measures at national and regional levels.

Its gender-mainstreaming strategy action plan commenced in 2009. There are also sector guidelines and frameworks for mainstreaming gender in trade, and measures to assess the gender distribution impact of trade through sex-disaggregated data, knowledge building and gender impact assessment. In 2017, it participated in an UNCTAD-organised gender and trade training programme.

ECOWAS: There is a plan of action on gender and trade 2005–2020. There is also a draft supplementary act on equal rights of women and men for sustainable development within ECOWAS. The plan of action includes animal products and fisheries. ECOWAS, like other regional economic communities, utilises workshops and expert meetings on gender and trade to explore the pertinent issues women and men face as part of the process of developing strategy and ensuring buy-in from stakeholders and member states on the issues (ECOWAS Commission 2013).

EAC: The Gender Equality and Development Act propagated by the community was adopted by the East African Legislative Assembly with effect from March 2017. Under this act government in the region commit to address barriers to gender inequality. Gender concerns are also to be integrated into trade policy. States are obligated to collectively promote the participation of women and men in regional trade agreements to deliver sustainable economic growth and integrate the gender dimension to pursue safety for women in cross-border trade.

Some Commonwealth countries are also involved in political dialogue, partnership and cooperation agreements and regional strategy documents which reference gender issues, for example the ACP–EU Partnership (Cotonou) Agreement preamble.

Cyprus, Malta and the UK, as members of the EU, are parties to a number of such dialogues and frameworks including the EU–Andean Political Dialogue Articles 6, 41 and 44 (cooperation in the field of gender), the EU–Central American Dialogue and EU–Mercosur Trade Agreement.

Commonwealth members of APEC (Australia, Brunei Darussalam, Canada, Malaysia, New Zealand, Papua New Guinea and Singapore) and the Association of Southeast Asian Nations (ASEAN: Brunei Darussalam, Malaysia and Singapore) are also involved in mainstreaming gender into trade activities, and this is also the approach followed in the APEC Forum.

At the global level, UNCTAD has been a primary institution working on gender and trade. Since 2011 UNCTAD's gender and development programme has undertaken studies on the impact of trade on women, implemented an online gender and trade course that has involved 19 countries, and launched a trade and gender toolbox (July 2017). With this toolbox, countries can assess the impact of trade policies on women and proactively develop flanking measures before such policies are implemented. It is now working on supporting the development of a database and statistical information on gender and trade.

However, some gender activists argue that what is needed is the integration of gender into the discussion and negotiation of trade agreements so that offensive and defensive interests can be protected and guarded against before trade agreements are adopted. At the same time, other gender activists are questioning the relative value of integrating gender into trade agreements that may have adverse impacts on sustainable development. For example, many women's groups are concerned about what they see as an 'instrumentalising' of gender to 'pinkwash' trade agreements, especially with regard to contentious issues such as e-commerce/digital economy and government procurement.

To date, gender has not been integrated into any Commonwealth country's trade agreements. But at the practical and programmatic level some Commonwealth countries have gone quite deeply into developing trade and gender programmes and policies at national and regional levels. An indicative illustration of these initiatives include:

- The East African Sub-Regional Support Initiative for the Advancement of Women (EASSI), a collaboration between individuals, NGOs, coalitions and networks in the Eastern Africa sub region committed to the advancement of women, which among other activities, are working on gender and trade issues, particularly across five border points, including on the borders of Kenya, South Sudan, Rwanda and Tanzania. Both EASSI and the 2016 Kampala Declaration flagged women's low participation in trade and entrepreneurship in East Africa (highlighting both the Beijing Platform's Strategic Objective 7 and SDG16)[10]. The Declaration noted that 'Women still experience barriers to trade differently from men and gender-sensitive policies can help ensure that female importers and exporters reap the same benefits from improved trade logistics as their male counterparts (Kampala Declaration, paragraph 2e.'

  Among other policy advocacy advances made in the Kampala Declaration participants committed themselves to 'advocate for gender-responsive trade policies, facilitation and regional integration to facilitate small-volume traders, many of whom are women, in order to access regional markets,' (Kampala Declaration, p.3). Participants at the colloquium that generated the declaration also committed to raising awareness and support for knowledge sharing in order to enhance activism for gender equality in the implementation of SDGs at grassroots level and to support efforts to mitigate the effects of climate change on women including but not limited to improved food security, increased accessibility, availability and affordability of water, renewable and sustainable energy, and other resources.

- Specific to economic empowerment and capacity-building, they argued for increased access to credit and markets in both the formal and informal sectors and within and between countries; efforts to upskill women for improved economic productivity and productive involvement in the agricultural value chain; and support for or strengthening of associations of women at all levels for easy access to credit and other opportunities.

- Trademark East Africa promotes capacity-building for women entrepreneurs to foster their participation in exports and enable women to take advantage of new opportunities. The key is to determine where women trade and to help develop business clusters that promote the defensive and offensive interests of women-owned SMEs as they relate to trade. This initiative is supported by the Netherlands and was in operation from October 2015 to October 2016. A second five-year phase, with US$10 million of funding, started in 2017. It targets 25,000 women traders, seeking to remove internal impediments to trade that are faced by women and to promote the voice and participation of women in export trade in East Africa.

- Chase Bank of Kenya recently provided US$25 million (KSh2.5 billion) to lend to women-owned SMEs in Kenya. This was sponsored by the International Finance Corporation credit line from its Women Entrepreneur Opportunity Facility. The expectation is that this will help to radically increase the percentage of women-owned SMEs with access to credit beyond the 7 per cent that now have such access.

At the global level, there has been increasing attention to integrating gender and women's empowerment concerns into multilateral trade and trade-related initiatives such as:

- Aid for Trade and the Enhanced Integrated Framework (the Aid for Trade mechanism that supports LDCs).

- The ITC's Women and Trade Programme and SheTrades global. The ITC is a 50-year-old joint agency of the World Trade Organization and the United Nations (UNCTAD) that seeks to help developing and transitioning countries improve their exports by implementing and delivering practical trade-related assistance projects. Through its Women and Trade programme, the ITC promotes inclusion of women-owned SMEs in trade. It does so through research and capacity-building on programmatic engagement, such as trade fairs/exhibits etc., with women-owned SMEs in developing and transitioning countries. The ITC seeks to connect women to markets and get women tapped into international trade. SheTrades Global is the premier global business event linking women entrepreneurs with buyers, partners, and investors. It focuses on business development, investment, and innovation. Through the SheTrades online platform that connects women entrepreneurs to buyers, sellers, investors and partners, it is reported to have generated over US$80 million worth of new business opportunities for women (ITC 2017).

- Declaration on Gender and Trade at WTO MC 11. At the 11th Ministerial Conference of the WTO, 118 WTO members and observers agreed to support the Buenos Aires Declaration on Women and Trade, a collective initiative to increase the participation of women in trade which seeks to remove barriers to, and foster, women's economic empowerment (WTO 2017b). It is expected that the outcome of this initiative will contribute to the SDGs, including achieving gender equality through the empowerment of women and girls (SDG5). The actions promised by the proponents of the agreement include finding 'ways to best tackle barriers to trade, lack of access to trade financing and sub-optimal participation of women in public procurement markets', 'exchang[ing] information about what has worked – and what has not – in their attempts to collect gender-disaggregated economic data and to encourage women's participation in the economy' and scrutiny of individual countries' 'own policies through a gender lens' (WTO 2017b). However, the declaration does not address trade rules and trade agreements.

3.1.2 One indicative case study of institutional approach to the integration of gender and trade in the Commonwealth: Uganda Gender and Export promotion

In 2009, Uganda launched its gendered national export strategy (NES, hereafter g_NES), which was developed from the 2007 National Export Strategy. It did this through a collaborative process which included multistakeholder consultations, the setting up of a gender strategy team that included stakeholders from NES priority sectors, and cross-sectoral support services. The g-NES was supported by the ITC. Four sectors were prioritised as the sectors that have the highest potential to mainstream gender and vulnerable groups into export trade: coffee, tourism, commercial craft and dairy.

Five weighted criteria were considered to arrive at the selection of these sectors:

1. sectors with contribution and relevance to national socio-economic goals, including greater participation of women in economy and export (30 %);
2. sectors where women have demonstrated a high potential for entrepreneurship/investment but are hampered by lack of finance, information and skill (25 %);
3. sectors with a high level of growth from international trade and where women are visible in the value chain (20 %);
4. sectors with high value addition by women (15 %);
5. sector where production resources are readily available but not equitably shared by men, women and vulnerable groups (10 %).

A detailed gender sensitive value-chain analysis of each sector was undertaken. The process of consultation on the g_NES took about five months and launched a three-year g_NES action plan for gendering the NES, including a financing strategy. The key principals that worked to design, implement and monitor the g_NES included a women's NGO, a women and trade group, the Uganda Export Promotion Board, the National Planning Authority, the National Bureau of Statistics, the ministries of agriculture, trade and industries, and the Private Sector Foundation.

Outcome/achievement(s)

It was expected that the g_NES would affect the next formulation of the country' NES. The g_NES was used to augment the NES of 2009–2012. Furthermore, the updated Coffee Export Strategy of 2012–2017 built on the g_NES. Particular inclusion of gender could be found in strategic area 1, the section on constraints to Uganda's competitiveness and a gender section. Discussion of gender issues was comprehensively integrated throughout the document, including the discussion of the g_NES findings and actions relative to the coffee sector. Overall, the coffee strategy was a quite comprehensive attempt to address or flag the key areas of intervention that are important for successful integration of gender and trade, such as statistics and databases (challenges and shortcomings); economic and trade policies; labour policies; fundamental complementary policies (such as education, security, social policies, childcare etc.); and gender policy (Uganda has had a gender policy since 1997).

Potential links to climate change and gender

The g_NES analytical profile sections for sectors included a category entitled 'environment', but this focused on occupational safety issues in the work and production environment. A future g_NES could very easily incorporate the category of climate change, identifying the impacts on the sector and its differential impacts on women and men as well as identifying the diversification and climate-proofing actions needed. The finance section could include reference to adaptation finance as part of its financing strategy.

Ultimately, gender-related commitments need to be tailored to the economic and political contexts of the countries involved. Gender and trade impact assessment tools could be very useful in providing information on sensitive sectors where trade liberalisation should be expedited, delayed (providing time for adjustment) or exempted with a view to enhancing or protecting female employment or female-owned enterprises. In the sectors identified as critical, professional training and educational policies and other measures should be put in place to upgrade women's skills and integration in markets and provide financing and technology that enable them to move to more competitive, higher value-added and higher-technology sectors of the economy.

At the same time, explicit references to gender equality in the core text of trade agreements could help increase the level of political commitment of key stakeholders. To date, such references in trade agreements (e.g., Chile–Uruguay (2016), Canada–Chile (1997 updated) and some EU agreements[11]) have a light touch, are not legally binding, do not incorporate much about international trade rules and avoid directly addressing the impacts of trade liberalisation on women.[12] It is possible that deepening of this trend could result in the increased availability of funding for gender-related programmes of technical cooperation, such as with the Aid for Trade framework as well as other trade related and capacity-building programmes. Such financing is critical for supporting the establishment of local research capacity in the developing world to conduct gender impact assessments of trade agreements, foster the collection of and construction of gender-disaggregated data bases, and further encourage both developed and developing countries' governments to take ownership of gender-related policy options, while enhancing economy-wide coverage of gender-related trade assessments.

3.2 Gender issues in climate governance[13]

Feminists and gender advocates working within the context of the UNFCCC negotiating space, under the umbrellas of the Women and Gender Constituency and the Global Gender and Climate Alliance (GGCA), as well as at national levels, have been hard at work seeking to promote gender-sensitive and gender-equal climate governance policies around adaptation, mitigation, technology development and transfer, climate finance and capacity-building. These activities are structured around at least five important pillars: (1) improving women's voice and agency in climate governance, through gender balance in representation and improved capacity-building for climate negotiations for women; (2) improving women's empowerment and gender analysis in climate and related sciences; (3) programmes and training to enhance the skill set of women to undertake adaptation, mitigation and related vulnerability assessments; (4) increasing women's participation in timely and strategic interventions around climate protection and building resilience; and (5) ensuring adequate climate finance, which is publicly sourced, non-debt-creating and easily accessible, to developing countries and community-based organisations in those countries, and ensuring gender equity in the flow of this finance. The fulcrum of the argument for entrenching a gendered approach within climate governance is based on a rights-based approach and rests on at least three foundational pillars.

Gender issues are important in climate protection policies, specifically in the design, implementation and financing of adaptation and mitigation strategies, for at least three main reasons:

1. Structural gender inequalities: these are affected by climate change, climate variability and the losses and damage they generate. The effects of extreme weather events as well as the long-term chronic impact of climate change on water, agriculture and natural resources affect pre-existing structural gender inequalities. Crises in health and food systems and the measures implemented to mitigate them can improve or worsen the situation for gender equality and women's social and economic empowerment.

2. Participation and democracy: the gendered nature of the economic and financial architecture that dominates the responses to climate change has implications for the participation of men and women in decision-making and affects men's and women's lives in different ways. Hence, it is important that women as well as men have a voice in decision-making on climate change policy, especially around adaptation and mitigation strategies. A high degree of integration of women's and men's participation and systemic representation (agency) across all aspects of climate governance is essential to ensure the fairest, equitable and cost-effective solutions to the climate challenge.

3. Accountability and monitoring: monitoring the gendered outcomes of climate change policy responses is important for pin-pointing reforms of climate protection systems so that adaptation and mitigation responses can promote gender equality, poverty eradication and sustainable development. Knowledge, experience, insights and capacities for contributing to the way forward require

drawing on all the available resources to which a country has access in a climate-constrained world. Women, indigenous peoples and other groups that have been historically marginalised have knowledge, insights and practices that could be integrated into climate protection policies. They also need the upgrading of their knowledge and capacities for ensuring livelihoods, for sustainable development and for contributing to local, national and planetary safety.

Gender and climate change is now embedded as an emergent part of the policy and operational arm of the global climate regime under the UNFCCC and related processes. Starting with a focus on promoting gender balance in decision-making, the Conference of the Parties (COP) of the UNFCCC set in place Decisions 36/CP.7 (2001, COP7) and 1/CP.16 (2010, COP16), both focused on improving the participation of women in the Convention's negotiation processes and in the representation of Parties in bodies established under the Convention.[14] These initial starting points were reinforced and enhanced by numerous (more than 60) decisions on gender and related topics in the priority/thematic areas under the Convention, culminating in the so-called gender decision of 2012 (23/CP.18; UNFCCC Secretariat 2015).

The gender decision adopted 'a goal of gender balance' in order to improve the participation of women in UNFCCC negotiations and in the representation of Parties in bodies established under the Convention and its Kyoto Protocol. The decision also began to broaden the scope of gender integration by saying that the gender balance would more effectively inform climate change policy that addresses the needs of women and men equally. It also referred to 'gender sensitive climate policy' and added the issue of gender and climate as a standing item on the agenda of the sessions of the Conference of the Parties (UNFCCC Secretariat 2015, p. 9).

In 2014, the Lima Work Programme on Gender (LPWG) was adopted (Decision 18/CP.20, COP20) in order to enhance the implementation of the decisions made up to 2014. This was the first broad-spectrum attempt to deepen the work on gender and climate and to move it beyond a simple emphasis on gender balance. The LWPG also sought to 'promote gender sensitivity in developing and implementing climate policy and to achieve gender-responsive climate policy in all relevant activities under the Convention' (para. 1 23/CP.18), and further proposed to 'clarify the meaning of the term "gender-responsive climate policy" from an implementation perspective' and improve the development and effective implementation of gender-responsive climate policy.[15] The Lima Decision was operationalised by establishing a two-year work programme on the two key issues of promoting gender balance and achieving gender-responsive climate policy to guide the effective participation of women.

The Lima Decision and its implementation involve multiple gendering aspects including training, awareness of female and male delegates of issues related to gender balance and climate change, capacity-building for female delegates, in-session workshops on gender-responsive climate policy vis-à-vis adaptation, mitigation, technology transfer and development. The decision also made the first steps towards the institutionalisation of gender mainstreaming by requesting that the Executive

Secretary of the UNFCCC appoint a senior gender focal point to develop and ensure an action plan for the LWGP's implementation. However, notably, the decision provided no additional resources for this.

The 2015 Paris Agreement (1/CP.21) reinforced work already under way. Preambular paragraph 11 exhorts parties to the agreement 'when taking action to address climate change [to] respect, promote and consider their respective obligations on human rights, the right to health, the rights of indigenous peoples, local communities, migrants, children, persons with disabilities and people in vulnerable situations and the right to development, as well as gender equality, empowerment of women and intergenerational equity'. Article 7, paragraph 5, acknowledges 'that adaptation actions should follow a country-driven, gender-responsive, participatory and fully transparent approach' and Article 11, paragraph 2, on capacity-building, states that 'capacity building should be guided by lessons learned and should be an effective, iterative process that is participatory, cross-cutting and gender-responsive'.[16]

The subsequent Marrakech Meeting of the Parties (COP22, 2016) not only extended the time frame of the LWGP but also sought to enhance and expand its scope by mandating the design of a gender action plan within the framework of the UNFCCC during the 2017–2018 period. (This sought to complement existing frameworks and instruments for gender mainstreaming, including gender action plans, in the UNFCCC's bodies and ancillary bodies, such as the Least Developing Countries Expert Group and the operating entities of the financial mechanism of the Convention, the Green Climate Fund (GCF) and the Global Environment Facility. Both of these last have gender action plans in operation.)

The UNFCCC Parties' Gender Action Plan (GAP) was adopted in 2017 and will be reviewed in 2019[17]. It will be the main instrument for further deepening the work on integrating gender into global and national climate policies, programmes and projects. Future meetings of the UNFCCC's Subsidiary Body on Implementation and the Subsidiary Body for Scientific and Technological Advice, and all other institutional frameworks, will link to the ongoing work of gender integration and gender-responsive climate policy through the GAP process as well as decision-making under the ambit of the Lima Work Programme and its future variants. The COP has also invited 2017 invited 'Parties, members of constituted bodies, United Nations organizations, observers and other stakeholders to participate and engage in implementing the gender action plan … with a view to advancing towards the goal of mainstreaming a gender perspective into all elements of climate action'. The process of further elaborating and implementing the GAP, both at the UNFCCC and at regional and national levels, is currently under way.

However, while the work on gender and climate change seems to be proceeding on track at the global level, at the regional, national and local levels there are still ongoing struggles to understand and adopt a gender and climate framework, especially when a trade dimension is raised. This is the case across all regions and countries of the Commonwealth. Section 3.3 explores these issues in that context.

The GAP (2017), created under the Lima Work Programme on Gender, seeks to advance women's full, equal and meaningful participation and promote gender-responsive climate policy and the mainstreaming of a gender perspective in the implementation of the Convention and the work of Parties, the Secretariat, United Nations entities and all stakeholders at all levels. The GAP recognises the need for women to be represented in all aspects of the UNFCCC process, and the need for gender mainstreaming through all relevant targets and goals in activities under the Convention as an important contribution to increasing their effectiveness. The GAP has five priority areas and lists the three or four activities in each that will drive the achievement of its objectives in 2018–2019. (These are: 1) Capacity-building, knowledge sharing and communication; 2) Gender balance, participation and women's leadership (2018–2019); 3) Coherence--strengthening the integration of gender considerations within the work of UNFCCC bodies, the secretariat and other United Nation entities and stakeholders towards the consistent implementation of gender-related mandates and activities; 4) Gender-responsive implementation and means of implementation (2018–2019) --ensure the respect, promotion and consideration of gender equality and the empowerment of women in the implementation of the Convention and the Paris Agreement and the promotion of gender-responsive access to finance in the implementation of climate; and 5) Monitoring and reporting (2018–2019) in terms of improving tracking in relation to the implementation of and reporting on gender-related mandates under the UNFCCC.

3.3 Gender and climate policy in Commonwealth developing countries

Incorporating a gender focus in public policy aimed at confronting and adapting to the impacts of climate change is still a grave and serious pending task in Commonwealth regions such as the Caribbean (Wedderburn and Grant Cummings, 2017). While Commonwealth countries, particularly SIDS and LDCs, participate actively in the coalition of the '1.5°C to stay alive' advocacy campaign, and have had notable success in influencing global policy regime, as evidenced by the incorporation of the 1.5°C limit, and loss and damage, in the Paris Agreement on Climate Change, these regions do not seem to be well versed in advancing gender and climate change issues locally, regionally or globally.

Moreover, gender assessments of the intended nationally determined contributions (INDCs, submitted to the UNFCCC in 2015), which become nationally determined contributions (NDCs) under the Paris Agreement, show uneven uptake of gender issues across the Commonwealth. (NDCs are to be implemented in 2020 and to be reviewed every five years.)[18] In general, (I)NDCs have weak integration of gender and other social concerns, including human rights and poverty eradication, and weak linkages with the 2030 Agenda on Sustainable Development or its SDGs (though some of the underlying frameworks such as adaptation and national climate change policies, where these exist, may integrate social consequences and concerns).

For example, among Caribbean countries, Guyana has quite a strong and straightforward human rights emphasis in its INDC. Caribbean INDCs are strong on agriculture and some do refer to vulnerable groups. Barbados, Dominica, Haiti, and St Vincent and the Grenadines do make reference to women and gender. St Vincent and the Grenadines flags that gender is part of the Pilot Program for Climate Resilience (PPCR)[19] and there is a gender-sensitive Disaster Response Management Initiative. Jamaica's INDC makes reference to community-based adaptation and vulnerable groups.

This is in contrast with Africa, where countries in the ECOWAS and COMESA regions are quite strong on the inclusion of gender issues in their INDCs. Cameroon and the Democratic Republic of Congo, for example, make quite detailed reference to gender issues such as women's participation, women's agency and women as drivers of change, rather than simply relegating women to the category of 'vulnerable'. The Women's Environment & Development Organization highlighted that Ghana's INDC quantifies the cost of the policy underlying its programme to increase the resilience of women to climate change, and Jordan's INDC commits to ensuring that financing mechanisms for mitigation and adaptation address the needs and conditions for implementation in relation to poor women (WEDO 2016).

Beyond the INDCs and a few emerging NAPs and related adaptation planning, integration of gender into national climate policy is slow going. This process is being more or less spearheaded at the regional level. For example, there are the African Working Group on Gender and Climate Change and the African Group of Negotiators, which both made submissions on gender and climate change in response to the call for submissions on a specific range of topics related to the theme in the context of the Lima Work Programme of the UNFCCC. Likewise, some Commonwealth countries, mostly in Africa (Ghana, Kenya, South Africa, Malawi, Nigeria and Uganda), some in Asia (Bangladesh, India and Sri Lanka), one Pacific SIDS (Vanuatu) and one in the Caribbean (Antigua and Barbuda) have also made submissions since 2013.[20] (Developed commonwealth countries such as Canada regularly respond to call for submissions on gender in the COP decisions.)

In addition, UN agencies such as UNDP and FAO are intensifying their work on gender at both national and regional levels. Both are working to gender (I)NDCs and as readiness climate finance delivery partners or accredited entities working with countries on NAPs and developing proposals to the GCF for pipelines of programmes for funding.

Based on methodology developed by the IUCN, about 13 countries (including Bangladesh and Zambia) with support from the IUCN have developed climate change and gender action plans (ccGAP), and 13 regional ccGAPs have been prepared (Aguilar et al., 2015).

Chapter 4 discusses the interaction between trade and climate and the implications for inclusive economic growth, trade and development strategies and women's empowerment in Commonwealth and developing countries.

> **Box 3.2 Snapshots of some national approaches to gender and climate change in Commonwealth countries**
>
> **Lesotho:** 2012–2017 National Strategic Development Plan integrates climate change and recognises gender inequality as a major challenge contributing to poverty.
>
> **Malawi:** National Adaptation Programme of Action and National Climate Change Policy have integrated gender as a cross-cutting issue.
>
> **Nepal:** mainstreams gender through its renewable energy sector, setting it apart as a leader on gender.
>
> **Pakistan:** has a Ministry of Climate Change. Its 2012 National Climate Change Policy includes gender among its ten objectives – 'to focus on pro-poor gender sensitive adaptation while also promoting mitigation to the extent possible in a cost-effective manner' – and moreover includes a subsection on gender that presents specific policy measures.
>
> **Tanzania:** national policy framework on gender and climate change is integrated into its National Climate Change Strategy and Second National Communication to the UNFCCC.
>
> **Uganda:** draft Climate Change Policy includes gender as a cross-cutting theme and highlights the importance of gender mainstreaming and gender responsiveness in all climate change adaptation and mitigation strategies, plans, budgeting and implementation of issues.
>
> **Sudan:** gender considerations are being integrated into forestry initiatives and REDD+ preparedness, planning and pilot projects.
>
> Source: Adapted from Aquilar et al. (2015).

Notes

1 This section draws heavily on Williams (2003, 2019a, b) and Carr and Williams (2010).
2 It is possible that increasing the de minimis threshold for levying duties (i.e. refraining from levying customs duties on goods below a certain value) could lead to increased trade in small packages that would benefit MSMEs' integration into GVCs, as is being discussed under the current e-commerce negotiations at the WTO (DIKH 2018).
3 There may be some downturn in this trend because, as noted by the ILO (2016), between 1995 and 2015 the participation of women in the labour force decreased from 52.4 per cent of the overall total to 49.6 per cent. It is not clear if this trend related to the agricultural sector in significant ways (FAO 2011).
4 The overall source of statistics in these paragraph is WTO (2017a).
5 Some researchers argue that if African countries had closed the gender gap in schooling, 1960–1992, as quickly as East Asia did, this would have almost doubled per capital income growth in the region (Klassen 2002, Birsdall et al.,1995). This gap between the potential and actual productivity of women and its cost to GDP is not just a developing-country phenomenon. According to the IMF, increasing women's participation in the labour market would raise the USA's GDP by 5 per cent, Japan's by 9 per

cent and Egypt's by 34 per cent. Kinoshita, Y., and Kochhar, K. (2016), https://www.imf.org/external/pubs/ft/fandd/2016/03/kinoshita.htm

6   GATI: Gender and Trade Initiative; IIFT: Indian Institute of Foreign Trade; RIS: Research and Information System for Developing Countries, CUTS International; CWS: The Centre for WTO Studies and their relationship to the work on gender and trade in India are discussed more fully in Ratna 2010a.

7   At least in the 2009–2013 period of India's FTP, two sectors employed more women than men: manufacture of tobacco products (66.89 %) and manufacture of wearing apparel, except fur apparel (60.88 %). There are several sectors where female employment is more than 30 per cent: agriculture and animal husbandry service activities, except veterinary activities (39.53 %); manufacture of footwear (36.8 %); manufacture of other food products (36.18 %); manufacture of watches and clocks (34.13 %); manufacture of knitted and crocheted fabrics and articles (31.56 %); television and radio receivers, sound or video recording or reproducing apparatus and associated goods (31.27 %); and other chemical products (30.46 %). Notably, there were high compound annual growth rates in percentages of female employment among directly employed workers: mining and quarrying (31.99 %); manufacture of other electrical equipment (10.42 %); and manufacture of optical instruments and photographic equipment (8.34 %). There were negative compound annual growth rates in percentages of female employment among directly employed workers in areas such as 'dressing and dyeing of fur; manufacture of articles of fur' (−59.59 %); and reproduction of recorded media (−23.31 %), Ratna (2010b, p.43 & 48).

8   For example, the Chile–Canada agreement includes 'a provision to enable the Gender Committee to work with other committees under the FTA to sensitize them to gender issues and considerations; including gender-based analysis and the collection of gender data as additional areas for cooperation; a strengthened institutional framework of the chapter in terms of reporting to the Free Trade Commission; and additional requirements concerning meeting frequency and public reporting' (Government of Canada 2018).

9   Technically, the successor to the trade part of the Cotonou Agreement is a self-contained agreement that currently still exists and is in the process of renegotiation. Gender and trade is likely to figure in the post-Cotonou agreement (PCA) after 2020 and hence the PCA could conceivably become the new 'gold standard' in this area. Thanks to Peter Lunenborg for bringing this very important point to my attention (Lunenborg, P., personal correspondence).

10 The Kampala Declaration on Women and the Sustainable Development Goals in East and Horn of Africa, October 2016. http://www.seatiniuganda.org/publications/downloads/92-kampala-declaration-on-women-and-the-sustainable-development-goals-in-east-and-horn-of-africa-october-2016/file.html (accessed 05 Sept 2019).

11 According to the European Parliament, only one in five EU trade agreements makes reference to women's rights, and only two in five include references aiming to promote gender equality. MEPs called for such provisions to be strengthened to promote women's rights and to improve women's working conditions in export-oriented industries (such as garment and textile manufacturing and agriculture) and argued that the European Commission should promote and support the inclusion of a dedicated gender chapter in all future EU trade agreements. They further argued that trade liberalisation should avoid contributing to the precariousness of labour rights and increased gender wage gaps (Press Releases FEMM INTA, 24-01-2018 - 14:35).

12 Other agreements with broad references to gender considerations include the following. (1) The Framework for the Integration of Women in APEC 1999 highlighted gender analysis of the deliberation of and recommendations of APEC, collection and use of sex-disaggregated data in APEC meetings and conferences, the promotion of the participation of women in the institutional framework of APEC and a practical guide for gender analysis, an ad hoc advisory group on gender integration to assist senior officials' meetings, and later the Women and the Economy Forum and at least two public-private dialogues on women in the economy. In addition, the APEC Secretariat has a Director of Gender Integration Programs (Frohmann 2017). (2) The ACP-EPA agreements 2000, revised 2005 and 2010, expiring in 2020, preamble, Articles 1, 9, 11, 20, 25, 31 and 31, affirms the International Convention on Women's Rights, flags that gender issues should be considered and gender should be mainstreamed in technical cooperation and development cooperation including

macroeconomic policies. (3) The CARIFORUM EPA 2008 also reaffirms issues such as decent work for all including women. (4) The EU–EAC EPA incudes an article on fisheries referring to poverty alleviation measures and the participation of marginal groups in the fishing industry, including gender equity in fishers and capacity development for women traders (Article 89(g) (ii)). (5) The Dominican Republic–Central America–US FTA 2005 on labour cooperation and capacity-building mechanisms includes gender-related issues (elimination of discrimination in respect of employment and occupation). The side agreement on labour cooperation flags the promotion of equality of women and men in the workplace (Article 11).

13 This section draws freely from Williams (2015, 2016, 2017, 2019a, b).

14 Decision 1/CP.16 is flagged here because it is given prominence in the preamble to the decision on the Lima Work Programme on Gender, but it makes only two references to gender: first, in the preamble, 'and notes the differential impacts of climate change on segments of the population, owing to the intersections such as age and gender'; and second, in the operative section on 'Shared Vision', where it recognises that gender equality and the effective participation of women are important for effective climate action on all aspects of climate change. For more in-depth treatment of these decisions please see UNFCCC Secretariat (2015).

15 Whereas the terms 'women', 'women's participation', 'gender balance' and 'gender composition' have been a part of the terminology of COP decisions since 2001, the phrase 'gender-sensitive climate policy' made its first appearance in the UNFCCC context officially in the 2012 gender decision, where the goal of gender balance was articulated with a view to 'advancing gender sensitive climate policy'. Following this, Decisions 1/CP.16, 5/CP.17, 12/CP.18 and 18/CP.19 (2013 COP19) also included reference to a gender-sensitive approach to national adaptation plans (NAPs). Gender-sensitivity also permeates discussions around NAPs in Decision 5/CPO.17 (2011, COP17) which makes reference to 'gender-sensitive approaches'. It can also be found in the Nairobi work programme on impacts, vulnerability and adaptation to climate change, Decision 6/CP.17, 2011, COP17, which also raised gender issues.

16 For example, the COP decisions on NAPs (5/CP.17, 2011, COP17) and on the Nairobi work programme both flag a gender-sensitive approach and gender issues in adaptation. The Cancun Agreement (1/CP.16, 2010, COP16) and Decision 15/CMP.7 (2011, CMP.7) under the Kyoto Protocol had both previously flagged that capacity-building should take into account gender aspects.

17 The GAP was mandated by 21.CP.21, paragraph 27, and is approved and annexed to Draft_CP.23. There is to be a synthesis report on the implementation of the GAP in 2019, and it will be reviewed at COP25, in the context of the review of the Lima Work Programme (21.CP22, paragraph 6).

18 Although the Paris Agreement is to be implemented through the vehicle of the NDCs, there is much uncertainty about the detail of the rules. The rules governing the NDCs are still being discussed in ongoing negotiations, especially with respect to areas of the agreement called Global StockTake and compliance. The so-called rulebook for the Paris Agreement, which will be explicit about the NDCs' time frame and substantive content, is expected to be negotiated by 2019 or 2020. The NDCs come into play in 2020 and are currently expected to have a five-year cycle.

19 The PPCR is a US$1.2 billion funding window of the World Bank's Climate Investment Fund for climate change adaptation and resilience building in developing countries.

20 Submissions from Parties to the COP in 2013: Advancing the goal of gender balance--, *Views from Parties on options and ways to advance the goal of gender balance in bodies*. Submissions to the subsidiary bodies 2015–2018: 1) Gender and Climate Change 2015, *Views on matters to be addressed at the in-session workshop on gender responsive climate policy with a focus on mitigation action and technology development and transfer*; 2) Gender and Climate Change 2016, *Views on matters to be addressed at the in-session workshops on gender-responsive climate policy with a focus on adaptation and capacity-building, and training for delegates on gender issues*; 3) Gender and Climate Change 2017, *Views on possible elements of the gender action plan to be developed under the Lima work programme on gender*; 4) A. Gender Action Plan, activity E.1, (Decision 3/CP.23), *Submissions from Parties and observers on the following, including sex disaggregated data and gender analysis, where applicable: (a) Information on the differentiated impacts of climate change on women and men, with special attention paid to local communities and indigenous peoples; (b) Integration of gender considerations into*

adaptation, mitigation, capacity-building, Action for Climate Empowerment, technology and finance policies, plans and actions; (c) Policies and plans for and progress made in enhancing gender balance in national climate delegations; and B. Gender Action Plan, activity A.2, *Submissions from Parties and observer organizations on the systematic integration of gender sensitive, and participatory education, training, public awareness, public participation and public access to information from national to local level into all mitigation and adaptation activities implemented under the Convention and the Paris Agreement, including into the implementation of NDCs and the formulation of long-term low greenhouse gas emission development strategies.*

Chapter 4

Exploring the Linkages Between the Governance of Climate Change and the Governance of International Trade[1]

Developing countries, whether landlocked developing countries (LLDCs) or SIDS, LDCs or low- to middle-income African, Asian, Caribbean or Latin American states, are the ones that suffer most from globalised market failures such as climate change, environmental degradation of the oceans and seas, loss of biodiversity, desertification, and economic and financial shocks emanating from the financial or trade system. Climate change and climate variability contribute to droughts and flooding, which adversely affect ecosystems, human health systems, food production and water availability, as well as posing challenges for economy-wide development pathways.

The relationship between trade and climate change is a complex nature. Trade physically affects climate change both directly, through GHG emissions generated by transport, and indirectly, through trade-induced growth affecting production and consumption. Global warming impacts trade, notably through its effect on agricultural production. Furthermore, policies aimed at the mitigation of climate change affect trade and, at the same time, trade policies can be used to address climate change. Climate change policy debates and specific measures to which or SIDS, LDCs is vulnerable are shaped by United Nations Framework Convention on Climate Change (UNFCCC) and World Trade Organisation (WTO) negotiations. Whether trade matters related to climate change should be dealt with within the UNFCCC, the WTO, or both remains a contested issue. It has been argued that the adoption of the Paris Agreement in 2015 'created a new context for the interface between climate change and trade policy' (Climate Strategies 2018). This is because, as highlighted above, 'various measures with trade consequences are contemplated in the national climate pledges (I/NDCs) put forward under the Agreement, and calls for trade measures have intensified'. Undeniably, this changing context draws attention to the role of the international trading system in the response to climate change, including the WTO as well as regional and plurilateral trade agreements. This chapter seeks to pinpoint those interactions, noting areas of conflict and areas of synergies for gender equality and women's empowerment.

It is indisputable that the impacts of climate change, the outcome of the Paris Agreement and the outcome of trade negotiations will affect, for better or worse, the success of the 2030 Sustainable Development Agenda. Climate change is increasingly a trade issue, and trade issues are also interlinked with climate change adaptation and mitigation responses. Climate change can damage soil and crop yields and infrastructure, and thwart domestic production of goods and services. Measures to mitigate the effects of climate change, such as carbon taxes, bunker fuel levies, so-called green subsidies, carbon-friendly labels and standards, and removing trade restrictions in the energy and forestry sectors, are directly related to provisions in trade agreements. Other measures in the NDCs of countries can have spillover effects on trade. Likewise, trade measures such as intellectual property rights (IPRs), market access provisions and disciplines on subsidies can affect climate measures, or even undermine climate goals. Furthermore, the linkage between climate change policies and trade-related policies forms a bridge between the climate regime and the trade regime. Both climate change and trade, in all their expressions, affect resource allocation and the potential to generate structural change, including equity and distributional challenges, which are development issues. Ultimately, there could be positive synergies and even co-benefits for economic development if climate actions are supported by trade (Bridges 2016).

In the new environmentally constrained context, developing countries must prioritise reducing emissions, reshaping the energy mix for industrial and agricultural production and household uses (mitigation), promoting adaptation and climate resilience, and economic diversification alongside their over-riding priorities and commitments to poverty eradication. It means that developing countries are not just challenged to seek to close gaps in productivity, infrastructure, income and technology with OECD countries, if they are not to be left behind, with their citizens continually migrating to the latter. Developing countries must also pursue a low-carbon development pathway. This they must do while also ensuring maximisation of employment, poverty eradication and the *just transition of the workforce.*

4.1 Trade issues in the climate governance framework

The UNFCCC is a critical feature of the rules-based multilateral system. Under its climate regime, the linkage to trade and climate issues has evolved over time, from an initial concern in the 1990s with unilateral trade measures and spill over effects of measures, to today's Paris Agreement and its comprehensive ambition to cap emissions as soon as possible and to decarbonise the global economy. The ambition of the Paris Agreement gave rise to concerns about deeper issues underlying the interlinkage between climate and trade such as carbon leakages.

While the Paris Agreement has no direct reference to international trade or to unilateral trade measures, the relevant articles of the convention that are relevant to trade concerns apply. And the agreement does affirm the area of response measures in the preamble, Article 4 (and paragraphs 33, 34 and 95 of the related decision that give effect to the agreement). Actions in the trade area fit under the response measure framework as much as does the direct stipulation against unilateral trade measures in the UNFCCC. Unilateral measures are an area where the UNFCCC has already drawn a red line of sorts in Article 3.5 of the Convention and Article 2.3 of the Kyoto Protocol, which provide that measures taken to combat climate change should not constitute a means of arbitrary or unjustifiable discrimination or a disguised restriction on international trade.

> **Box 4.1 The Convention and the Kyoto Protocol**
>
> Recognition of trade as an issue relevant to the climate change regime started in 1992, with trade reflected in the principles of the Convention and later the Kyoto Protocol.
>
> *Article 3.5 stated that 'Parties should cooperate to promote ... an open economic system'. It also recognised that 'measures taken to combat climate change, including unilateral ones, should not constitute a means of arbitrary or unjustifiable discrimination or a disguised restriction on international trade'.*
>
> *The Kyoto Protocol,* **Article 2.3**, *stated that Parties included in Annex I should 'strive to implement policies and measures implemented under this Article in such a way as to minimize adverse effects including adverse effects of climate change, effects on international trade and social, environmental and economic impact on other Parties'.*

Some unilateral-type measures, such as attempts to implement aviation and shipping emission levies in the EU's emissions trading scheme, are being considered in fora such as the International Maritime Organization and the International Convention on Civil Aviation, but are not yet well developed in the WTO. Other issues such as carbon border measures have also yet to be adequately tackled by the WTO.[2] To date, there have been no significant disputes and hence no WTO or FTA rulings that relate to the fundamentals of climate protection/laws and policy tools:[3] funding mechanisms/programmes, carbon and other taxes, emission-trading systems (such as that of the EU), prohibition, international standards, financial instruments (such as the clean development mechanism or REDD+).

4.2 Climate issues and trade governance

The World Trade Organisation is the premier organisation dealing with trade issues at the global level. Therefore, any formal interface between trade and climate change would tend to take place under the auspice of the global governance entity supervising the multilateral trade system. Independently, of course, national governments through their bilateral and regional trade arrangements may elect to include climate issues, gender and other social issues as they desire. But multilateral enforcement of these issues must first be discussed and agreed at the WTO. For example, the Uruguay Round of negotiation focused on sewage services, refuse disposal services and sanitary services, and the environmental service sector is part of the Services Sectoral classification list. There are many WTO provisions that link to environment and climate change in sectoral issues such as around subsidies and domestic support in the agriculture sector but also in the energy sector.

The institutional governance structure of the WTO that is related to environmental issues includes but is not limited to:

- the Committee on Trade and Environment (CTE; the UNFCCC participates in its meetings);
- special sessions of the CTE (the UNFCC is an ad hoc observer);
- the Committee on Technical Barriers to Trade (discusses technical regulations adopted by governments to mitigate climate change, such as product standards and labelling requirements targeted at energy efficiency or emission control notified to WTO).

In addition, the WTO attends UNFCCC meetings of the COP.

Climate change is not part of the WTO's ongoing work programme, per se, nor are there any WTO rules specific to climate. While the goal of the international trade system, as supervised by the WTO, is trade liberalisation and economic growth in the context of citizens' welfare and the optimal use of the world's natural resources, the main goal of the UNFCCC-led climate regime is to promote and ensure the prevention of dangerous climate change. But it does that in the context of environmental protection/preservation of the ecosystem and sustainable development. Sometimes these sets of goals may collide with each other. Climate mitigation requirements can affect trade competitiveness, and trade measures such as IPRs may impact the flow of environmentally sound technologies. This could also be the case with border carbon adjustment measures and the application of subsidies to green technologies.

According to David Shark, WTO Deputy Director-General, it is 'critically important to ensure that the outcomes of our respective processes fully support each other's so as not to miss unique opportunity to usher in a new era of sustained and inclusive economic growth, social development and environmental protection,' (Shark 2015). Shark said that international trade and the WTO can bolster efforts to combat climate change and to achieve sustainable development (ibid). In this context, it is important to note that paragraph 31 of the Doha Ministerial Declaration acknowledges the agreement to negotiations on the relationship between existing WTO rules and specific trade obligations set out in multilateral environmental agreements.

In general, researchers argue that there are three avenues through which WTO can assist global climate change efforts.

First, the chapter on trade and environment is part of the Doha Round of negotiations.

Second, the WTO institutional framework of rules can assist global efforts on climate change, since some provisions in WTO rules are related to key mitigation measures adopted by governments such as carbon taxes, carbon-friendly labels and standards, and green subsidies, box shifting aside. In addition, the WTO's promotion of transparency, mutual understanding and cooperation on trade and trade-related issues can be an example of transparency.

Third, trade and environmental negotiations are ongoing. One example is the CTE, which serves as a forum for constructive dialogue on the links between trade and the environment. The CTE has discussed matters relevant to climate change, the benefits of removing trade restriction in the energy and forestry sectors, and the effects of carbon foot-printing on the market access opportunities of developing countries. The Committee on Technical Barriers to Trade works on transparency. It has undertaken discussion on energy-efficient labelling etc.

Trade policies can be used to maximise the spread of climate-related technologies through elimination of tariffs and NTBs on environmental goods and services. Trade policy is, therefore, suggested as a mechanism to facilitate compliance and participation in global mitigation and also supplement domestic measures to internalise the cost of climate distortions. In particular, trade policy is considered to have four roles under a global climate regime (De Melo and Mathys 2010): address leakage and competitiveness issues; generate sanctions against non-participation and non-compliance; help reach global efficiency in mitigation policies by facilitating the separation of abatement location and the bearer of the cost of abatement; and, finally, maintain a free trade regime, which is crucial for technology transfers and trade policies that can be used to maximise the spread of climate-related technologies through elimination of tariffs and NTBs on environmental goods and services.

Box 4.2 Issues linking trade and climate

- Carbon markets – carbon is traded as a commodity, e.g. in emissions trading.

- Response measures – these are measures put in place to address climate change that can have an adverse impact on the social and economic development of other countries.

- Agriculture – the agriculture sector has experienced and will continue to feel the effects of climate change. This therefore has an impact on trade in agricultural products.

- Bunker fuels – these are fuels used in international transport, particularly maritime shipping and aviation. Regulation of emissions from these sources has a direct impact on the cost of moving goods and people, which has an impact on trade. SIDS, usually in remote locations, would be particularly vulnerable to higher transport costs.

- Technology – IPRs are seen by some as barriers to technology transfer, deployment and diffusion.

WTO rules may be relevant to measures aimed at mitigating climate change. These include:

- Disciplines on tariffs (border measures), essentially prohibiting members from collecting tariffs at levels greater than that provided for in their WTO scheduled consolidation

- A general prohibition against border quotas. These are measures such as import bans or quotas that restrict quantities selectively. In order to ensure predictability, stability and fair play, the GATT has provisions that discourage the use of quotas and other measures used to set limits on quantities of imports (e.g. Article XI:1); these may include climate-motivated direct import bans (Westberg 2010).

- A general non-discrimination principle, consisting of the most-favoured-nation and national treatment principles.

- Rules on subsidies. Simply put, subsidies are direct payments to market actors. In general, more precise definition and rules on subsidies are in the WTO Agreement on Subsidies and Countervailing Measures and in the agreement on agriculture.[4] Increasingly, in the climate context, there are challenges to some WTO members' renewable energy subsidies, though other climate-related subsidies such as feed-in tariffs are seen to be compatible with WTO rules.[5]

- Rules on technical regulations and standards, which may not be more restrictive than necessary to fulfil a legitimate objective. Technical regulations and standards must also respect the principle of non-discrimination and be based on international standards, where they exist. There are also specific rules for sanitary and phytosanitary measures which are relevant for agricultural products.

- Disciplines relevant to trade in services, imposing general obligations such as most-favoured-nation treatment, as well as further obligations in sectors where individual members have undertaken specific commitments.

- Rules on trade-related intellectual property rights. These rules are relevant for the development and transfer of climate-friendly technologies and know-how.

Source: WTO (n.d.).

4.3 Linkages between climate change and trade – relevance for inclusive sustainable growth and women's empowerment

The synergies and dissonances between trade and climate discussed above have serious implications for inclusive economic growth, trade and development strategies and women's empowerment in developed and developing Commonwealth countries. The core of the SDGs revolves around the issues of poverty eradication, gender equality, food security/nutrition and access to water/sanitation/modern energy, benefiting from the oceans, seas and biodiversity etc. Climate change can have adverse impacts on these, as discussed in Chapter 2. But measures to address unsustainable development drivers to mitigate climate change can also adversely affect some of these goals unless care is taken to offset the negative impact. Trade can also directly adversely affect these core SDGs and influence their implementation in a way that precludes or restrains measures to address climate change if the measures seem to impact adversely on the trade sector. For example, increasing agricultural trade on a business-as-usual basis can lead to decreasing forest cover as well as increasing emissions from air freighting. Overall, trade intensification, which fosters growth, can inadvertently contribute to exacerbation of environmental and climate challenges.

At the very basic level, the trade regime's overall purpose is the expansion of international trade, which often requires cutting back on government interventions that inhibit trade expansion. On the other hand, as stated in the objective of the United Nations Framework Convention, the climate regime's basic purpose is the 'stabilization of greenhouse gas concentrations in the atmosphere at a level that would prevent dangerous anthropogenic interference with the climate system' and this will often require greater government regulation of private behaviour and actions.

The underlying framework agreed in Rio 1992 is that sustainable development is the approach for both areas, and equity is the underlying principle to reconcile the two worlds when trade and environmental actions are in conflict. The 27 Rio Principles wrestled with the important reality that the trade regime and the climate change regime are two distinct worlds, whose overlapping areas may lead to conflicting policies. In fact, the provisions of the UNFCCC illustrate very well the ways in which such conflicts can be resolved.

Presenting the SDG report 2017, the UN Secretary-General postulates that climate action plays a central role in achieving the SDGs. He argues that the interlinked challenges of climate change and sustainable development must be urgently addressed to deliver a stable and secure world to future generations. 'We need to recognize that climate change became the main accelerator of all other factors,' said Mr Guterres, emphasising the need to address climate change in order to successfully achieve the SDGs. 'Climate change presents the single biggest threat to sustainable development everywhere and its widespread, unprecedented impacts disproportionately burden the poorest and most vulnerable' (United Nations n.d.).

The Paris Agreement marks a new era for international climate action in general, and specifically for international carbon markets. Though the agreement does not mention markets per se, Article 6, paragraph 4, establishes what has become to be known as the Sustainable Development Mechanism, which builds on and shares some features of the Kyoto flexible mechanisms, namely the Clean Development Mechanism and joint implementation.

UNFCCC measures are focused around addressing unsustainable drivers of development (such as monoagriculture, aspects of industrial agriculture and production, deforestation and overexploitation of fisheries). Therefore, climate policies in developing countries must be aligned with the SDGs and hence pursue sustainability in the short, medium and long terms. There is certainly an imperative for coherence in the pursuit of climate policies in the context of sustainable development given the need for almost certain drastic changes in economic activities including energy generation, agriculture, land use, transport, services etc. (UNCTAD 2015). Markets will also need to be strengthened to allow the scaling up of innovation, production and deployment of sustainable energy technologies (UNCTAD 2015).

4.3.1 The UNFCCC and sustainable development

The principles of equity and sustainable development are the core and pillars of the Convention. Article 3(4) states that 'The Parties have a right to, and should, promote sustainable development. Policies and measures to protect the climate system against human-induced change should be appropriate for the specific conditions of each Party and should be integrated with national development programmes, taking into account that economic development is essential for adopting measures to address climate change.'

The seventh and eighth items in the preamble to the Paris Agreement say '*Emphasizing* the intrinsic relationship that climate change actions, responses and impacts have with equitable access to sustainable development and eradication of poverty' and '*Recognizing* the fundamental priority of safeguarding food security and ending hunger, and the particular vulnerabilities of food production systems to the adverse impacts of climate change' (italics in original).

Implementation of the Paris Agreement is essential for the achievement of the sustainable development goals and provides a roadmap for climate actions that will reduce emissions and build climate resilience.

4.3.2 The WTO and sustainable development

The Marrakesh Agreement, which created the WTO, 'established a clear link between sustainable development and disciplined trade liberalization – in order to ensure that market opening goes hand in hand with environmental and social objectives' (WTO 2019). In the Doha Round, WTO members further pledged to 'pursue a sustainable development path with the launch of the first multilateral trade and environment negotiations,' (WTO 2019). The Doha Round thus directly embraced sustainable development and so can contribute positively to efforts to mitigate and adapt to climate change (WTO). However, the Doha Round is moribund and the current focus on the liberalisation of environmental goods and services may or may not necessarily support sustainable development or benefit poor women and men in developing countries. Though proponents of the reduction or elimination of import tariffs and NTBs on these goods and services may argue that it will have positive effects, including improved energy efficiency and positive impacts on the quality of water, soil and natural resources conservation, this may not unambiguously be the case.

Hence, critics of unbridled trade expansion, including some women's groups, are not convinced that trade will not adversely impact the outcome of climate policies. They make the case that, while international trade may contribute, for example, to reducing prices of solar water heaters, tanks for the production of biogas etc., it may also at the same time have adverse impacts on natural resources and ecosystems. There are concerns about the impacts on natural resources, which are not precluded from such liberalisation. Increased trade opportunities may lead to increased supply of products whose production makes intensive use of natural resources. In addition, in many urban areas of developing countries, women and men are intensively involved in sanitation, sewage and refuse disposal services, which, because of the liberalisation of government procurement, might put them at a disadvantage as workers and MSMEs, as they may be in danger of losing such niche markets.

On the other hand, eliminating tariffs and NTBs and reducing agricultural support in developed countries could positively affect men and women in the sector in developing countries.

This is offset by concerns about the projected increase in trade in bioethanol and the related impact on food production. In addition, increased discipline on the products used in biofuel production (i.e. which are classified under Harmonised System Code 2207) could adversely affect the domestic economy, not least because of the lack of availability of climate smart alternative energy sources at a competitive price. Therefore, some gender advocates seek to see more attention paid to integrating gender and climate issues in the trade policy framework and arrangements.

4.4 Gendering the trade–climate policy nexus[6]

Strategic interventions to integrate gender issues and concerns into policies, projects and programmes that address both climate change and trade are not very prominent, but it is increasingly being recognised that it is important to understand them and address the interlinkages. The scope for such interventions can be undertaken by a variety of institutions at the micro (household, individual and community), meso (sectoral and local government) and macro (national, regional and global) levels. These interventions range from specific gender actions and gender action plans to integrating gender in the provisions of climate agreements as well as in trade agreements, projects and programmes to empower women in communities, women-owned SMEs and individual women workers and managers of households. In some areas, regional institutions, such as the SADC, have protocols which include gender and environment interlinkages that could be further elaborated on, to integrate in a dynamic way the interlinkages between gender, climate and trade. Elsewhere, there are a growing number of initiatives to provide finance and credit to women-owned SMEs and to ensure that women's groups have access to climate finance.

Institutional frameworks to integrate gender are discussed in prior sections of this report, including direct and indirect references to gender and gender issues in final output documents (agreements and frameworks); the creation of gender units or gender focal points within the secretariats of the relevant authorities; and expert and policy dialogue meetings, national, regional and global, on the topic of gender and trade or gender and climate or the nexus of all three. Many of these efforts are hamstrung by the challenge of finding reliable gender-disaggregated data. In addition, there has been no significant effort to explore institutionally the link between gender, trade and climate. The areas where this may be closest to commencing are agriculture, food security and clean energy. However, at this time, there is no clear effective institutional framework for overseeing this triple linkage –trade, gender and climate – locally, nationally, regionally or globally.

This section provides an overview of efforts that seek to directly or indirectly integrate (a) gender and trade and (b) gender and climate change. ('Indirectly' refers to broad approaches that include references to social conditions and rights, indigenous peoples and labour conditions and rights.) It considers how these could be merged to address the gender–climate–trade interface. A general overview is presented which highlights the agreements (in the case of trade, either regional or free trade agreements), institutions and institutional frameworks, and the mechanisms and instruments. Lastly, where they are known, it identifies the possible achievements and outcomes. The section ends with indicative cases, one in each area (trade and gender, and climate and gender).

4.4.1 Institutional approaches to integrating gender, trade and climate change

As noted in earlier sections of this report, the work on gendering climate change at the institutional level, at least globally, is intensifying, with parties to the UNFCCC having adopted a GAP and including a gender focal point in the institutional framework. A similar process has been ongoing within the financing institutions for climate change. At this time, most all climate finance institutions have some provisions relating to gender issues, a gender policy and/or a GAP. These include the CIF of the World Bank, the Adaptation Fund and the Green Climate Fund.

Some national governments have also, to different degrees, integrated gender into the INDCs submitted to the UNFCCC for the Paris Agreement. A few Commonwealth countries also referenced both sustainable development and trade aspects in their INDCs, though this is not necessarily linked to the gender aspects. For example, India cites the imperatives of meeting the challenge of poverty eradication, food security and nutrition, universal access to education and health, gender equality and women's empowerment, water and sanitation, energy and employment in its INDC, but makes no reference to international trade. Jamaica flags 'people' and 'vulnerable groups' but did not address trade aspects. Nigeria made a small reference to trade in the context of the impact of the decline in world oil prices on its export revenue and hence government budget (Gov. Nigeria, 2015, p.1). It also references gender and social inclusion among the criteria against which potential mitigation actions are assessed. It also notes that climate change adaptation is an integrated component of sustainable development, and that the measures included in its INDC are 'deemed, at a minimum, to be gender neutral and/or to enhance social inclusion', (Gov. Nigeria, 2015, p.16). Barbados's INDC argues that gender and youth play a central role in the draft national climate change policy framework as well as being cross-cutting aspects of national development planning (Gov. Barbados, 2015, p.3). Barbados is one of few countries that flag gender equality issues in their mitigation section. It highlights that gender equality is key to building human capacity in both the sustainable energy and ICT sectors (ibid, p.8). Ghana's INDC promotes resilience for gender and the vulnerable as one of its priority policy actions, particularly through the implementation of community-led adaptation and livelihood diversification for vulnerable groups. It makes no mention of international trade. In its INDC, Kenya speaks of strengthening the adaptive capacity of the most vulnerable groups and communities through social safety nets and insurance schemes. In this context, it argues that, in addressing climate change issues, 'public entities are required to undertake public awareness and consultations and ensure gender mainstreaming, in line with the Constitutions and the climate change bill 2014', (Gov. Kenya, 2015, p.7)

According to its INDC, this is also the case for Sierra Leone[7]. For Kenya, climate and trade is implicitly considered through the aim of enhancing the resilience of the tourism, agriculture, livestock and fisheries value chains (the last two through the promotion of climate-smart agriculture).

Seychelles is one of very few countries that in their INDCs directly link climate change and trade aspirations. For Seychelles, climate mitigation is seen as an outcome or by-product of decreasing the country's dependence on imported fossil fuel and to 'enhance its balance of trade profile' (through a reduction in its energy bill) (Republic of Seychelles, 2015, p.9). Gender issues are flagged in the INDC. It notes that a stakeholder workshop highlighted 'that improved gender-sensitive capacity building, research and education was needed to underpin all climate change adaptation efforts in order to make them effective and resilient' (Rep of Seychelles, p.4). The INDC further noted that Seychelles' long-term vision… is nested in the country's broader aspiration of sustainable development: finding strategies to realise the nation's economic, social and cultural potential through an innovative, knowledge-led and gender-sensitive approach' (ibid, p.5). According to the INDC, in the long term, the Seychelles aim to '(b)uild gender-sensitive capacity and social empowerment at all levels to adequately respond to climate change' (ibid). South Africa's INDC, like those of many other African countries, flags gender considerations as part of its national climate change adaptation strategy and plan, but does not make a direct link to international trade.

Zambia's INDC makes quite a few direct references to gender issues but no direct reference to trade. For example, it seeks to promote conservation/smart agriculture leading to adaptation benefits and enhancing climate resilience, especially in rural areas, and thereby to contribute to poverty reduction 'particularly among women and the youth', Gov. Zambia, 2015, p.3). In seeking to promote the switching from conventional and traditional energy sources to sustainable and renewable energy sources and practices, the government states that 'it aims to improve health impacts due to child and maternal mortality and to improved education impact and the creation of opportunity for girls and women's education,' (Gov. Zambia (2015), p.4). Section 7.5, Gender, Youth and Vulnerable Groups Imperatives of Climate Change of Lesotho's NDC emphasises that the 'adaptation interventions proposed in this NDC are meant to a) recognize and respond to the differentiated needs, experiences, priorities and capacities of women and men; b) enhance gender balance and inclusiveness in various adaptation programmes and projects', LMS (2017, p.27).

Among African countries, the strongest reference to gender and climate change were to be found in the INDCs of Uganda and Zimbabwe both of which emphasise mainstreaming gender responsive climate policies as cross-sectoral aspect of the INDC contributions.

Among Asian commonwealth countries few reference trade or gender in their INDCs. India, while not referencing international trade, does make the point that its INDC contribution is based on its commitment to gender equality and women's empowerment among seeking to fulfil other aspects of the SDGs and sustainable development. Sri Lanka made reference to inclusivity relating to gender, youth and vulnerable groups and the ambitiousness of its targets. Both Malaysia and Singapore made reference to international trade context or situated their INDCs contribution somewhat in this framework. For example, Malaysia flagged that its INDC contribution was in the context of potential growth in the share of exports and increased food production. Pakistan stated that it anticipates its trade and industrial process to increase and with it growth in emissions; this is linked overall positive outcome from the China-Pakistan Economic Corridor (Gov. Pakistan, 2015, p.25). Sri Lanka discussed that its export crops, which are crucial for its foreign income, are sensitive to weather fluctuations. Singapore has the most extensive discussion linking its INDC and international trade. It flagged its carbon efficiency by highlighting that though its contribution to global trade was approximately 2.3%, its emissions was 0.11% (Gov. Singapore, 2015, p.3).[8]

There was no reference to either trade or gender issues in the INDCs of developed commonwealth countries such as Australia, Canada, New Zealand. (The UK is included with the EU's INDC contribution.)

Since INDCs, which become NDCs under the Paris Agreement, are to be revised every five years, there is considerable scope for both integrating trade dynamics (opportunities, challenges and constraints) into them and consolidating the initial gender dimensions. This is also the case for NAPs, the main tool for addressing adaptation issues. Adaptation planning processes are now being undertaken in many Commonwealth countries. These are not finite processes but are on a rolling basis, to take into account the changing nature of climate impacts. Fortunately for the uptake of gender analysis, the NAPs, according to the NAPs technical guidelines, have gender components. These are also highlighted in many of the INDCs in discussions around adaptation, and the framing of INDCs in national development context, such as those of Papua New Guinea, Uganda, and Zimbabwe. Furthermore, approval of funding proposals for NAPs by the GCF is linked to the inclusion of gender issues and environmental and social safeguards. NAPs in process to date, however, are not integrated with the regional or multilateral trade situations that Commonwealth countries face. However, as with the (I)NDC framework above, there is scope to integrate trade dynamism into the vulnerability and sectoral gap assessments that are core to the development and implementation of NAPs.

Notes

1 This chapter draws on Khor et al. (2017) and Khor (2010).
2 However, they relate to well-established WTO provisions such as GATT Articles I (MFN), XI and XX. Issues around technology transfer relate to the WTO TRIPS Agreement and disputes on subsidisation of renewable energy relate to the WTO agreement on subsidies and countervailing duties. Further clarification of the environment/climate–trade dimensions of these issues come under the Doha-mandated negotiations on trade and environment as elaborated in the Doha Declaration para 31.
3 However, it could be reasonably be argued that *Canada – Measures relating to the Feed-in Tariff Program* (DS426) can be considered a major case relating to climate change (Lunenborg, P., personal correspondence). Please see https://www.wto.org/english/tratope/dispu e/cases e/ds426 etm.
4 According to Howse (2010), the definition of 'subsidy' in Article 1 of the Agreement on Subsidies and Countervailing Measures means it must entail a 'financial contribution': governmental financial

assistance to firms, from cash payments through equity infusions to the provision of goods and services below market prices. It must also confer a 'benefit' on an enterprise and it must be 'specific', either de jure (legally targeted at a particular industry or enterprise or group of industries or enterprises) or de facto (in fact used only or disproportionately by a particular industry, enterprise, or group of industries or enterprises). Article 2.1(b) of the Agreement refines the concept of specificity.

5   For more on renewable energy subsidies see Howse (2010) and Mattoo and Subramanian (2013). Mattoo and Subramanian (2013) argue that 'carbon taxes (or cap-and-trade) are incontrovertibly WTO compatible because they are domestic in nature and trade-neutral.' Similarly, WTO rules do not constrain subsidies for clean energy such as feed-in-tariffs, now commonly used in several countries. Because their benefits are economy-wide, they would be considered non-specific and hence fall in the category of permissible subsidies (citing Hufbauer et al. 2009; Mattoo and Subramanian 2013; Mavroidis 2007).

6   This section draws freely on Williams (2019a,b).

7   Sierra Leone' INDC explicit flags gender perspective as a key input into its planning process. It highlights that '(p)illar eight (8) of Sierra Leone's five-year development plan considers Gender and Women's Empowerment. Therefore, in addressing climate change issues, public entities are required to undertake public awareness and consultations, and ensure gender mainstreaming,' (Govt. Sierra Leone, 2015, p.5).

8   According to its INDC, total trade in goods and services is 350% of Singapore's GDP, (Gov. Singapore, 2015, p.7).

Chapter 5

Summary, Recommendations and Way Forward[1]

5.1 Summary

The integration of gender into the climate–trade–sustainable development nexus will require both intensive actions focused on single areas in each sphere as well as joint actions across multiple streams of climate and trade policy, research, project and programme activities. Fortunately, some of this work is well under way within each separate domain, and even more so at sectoral (e.g. agriculture, forestry, energy) levels. The case for mainstreaming gender into trade policy and practice and into climate change is fairly well established, as indicated in the previous chapters of this report. Likewise, as also indicated earlier, the central importance of gender equality and women's empowerment concerns for the SDGs and overall sustainable development, as well as the processes for the implementation of SDGs, is also well established and engaging the strong actions of gender activists and gender focal points within civil society organisations, NGOs, UN agencies and other interested stakeholders.

UN Women has published a flagship report on the topic, *Turning promises into action: Gender equality in the 2030 agenda for sustainable development* (UN Women 2018). Other examples include the work of the UN High Level Panel on Women's Economic Empowerment; various subject matter gender champions; and the World Economic Forum's 'Closing the Gender Gap' project. The Commonwealth Secretariat is well versed in the progress of implementing policies and programmes on gender equality and sustainable development.[2] The African Union's Agenda 2063 also places a central focus on achieving gender parity.[3] ECOWAS members have focused on 'Challenges to Empowering the West African Woman and Girl-child vis-à-vis Political Participation and Employment Issues: one of the priorities of the ECOWAS Vision 2020'. In addition to the ongoing review and alignment of the SADC Protocol on Gender and Development with the post-2015 SDGs and targets, Agenda 2063 and the Beijing Declaration and Platform for Action, the SADC secretariat is seeking to develop the Regional Multi-Dimensional Women's Economic Empowerment Programme. In addition, the SADC's Revised Regional Indicative Strategic Development Plan and its Industrialisation Strategy and Roadmap, as noted by the Executive secretary, highlight 'the urgent need to mainstream gender and contribute to gender equality and equity,' (SADC 2016). Moreover, complementary to these institutional actions, a variety of think-tanks and the business community are engaging in promoting women's empowerment and sustainable development issues.

There are two weak points in this otherwise overall positive momentum: (1) the linkage between climate and trade and (2) the full integration of gender concerns in the overlapping aspects of the two domains. Data remain a formidable challenge in both domains. The challenge is how best to manage their integration with each other to effectively promote gender equality, women's empowerment and sustainable development. Can the goals and objectives of the gendering processes in the two spheres cohabit effectively or will they clash, confuse and distort? This remains to be seen. But there are common entry points to this joint integration.

First, drawing on the literature and points of views of the gender advocates in each area, it can be seen that the overarching goals of gender-responsive climate, trade and development policies are to:

- promote and ensure gender equitable results that improve the economic and social situation of men and women and promote women's empowerment;
- improve the welfare impacts of adaptation and mitigation strategies on men and women in communities across the developing world while increasing women's employment and trading opportunities at the sectoral level.

These can be achieved by setting in place processes and mechanisms to:

- improve the understanding of the primary, secondary, direct and indirect roles and contributions of women and men in adaptation and mitigation and how they relate to the trade sector;
- show how adaptation and mitigation policies affect women's and men's multiple roles as workers, producers, parents, caregivers and consumers (highlighting the differential constraints, challenges and opportunities of each gender in these areas), and show how women's trade and trade-related actions, including their capacity to take advantage of trade opportunities, are affected and can be addressed;
- ensure that climate protection policy and any trade interface have gender-based analytical components;
- show the particular impacts of climate change on sectors such as agriculture, fisheries, forestry, energy and tourism, and how these impacts have gender-differentiated outcomes;
- embed climate-focused gender analytical tools (that are relevant to both climate and trade policy) into global, regional and national climate protection policies as well as trade and development programmatic, support and capacity-building frameworks;
- ensure that climate change adaptation and mitigation policies, programmes and strategies aim to support the elimination of gender gaps and other social gaps, promote women's and men's wellbeing and enhance women's opportunity to trade, and ensure the proactive extension of such tools and frameworks to include trade aspects.

5.2 Recommendations and way forward

A process for forging a common understanding of what constitutes gender-responsive climate policies linked to trade and export promotion policies must be set in place.

Critically, gender advocates and gender machineries in the various sub regions must identify the strategic priorities and/or thematic issues that must be confronted in each sub regional and national context, in accordance with specific timelines and national circumstances. In gearing up for the processes of reviews of policies and programmes, especially around the review of NDCs, knowledge will need to be enhanced, as will the development of institutional capacity. In the climate policy arena, governments will need to prioritise enhancing knowledge and building institutional capacity both through their access to the GCF's Readiness and Preparatory Support Programme[4] and under the Paris Committee on Capacity-building.[5] In the realm of trade policy, Aid for Trade, the Enhanced Integrated Framework, and trade-related capacity-building and technical assistance will need to be enhanced to incorporate providing support to women entrepreneurs to address climate-related risks and undertake climate-proofing of trade infrastructure so they can be better able to sustainable participate in international trade activities either as single entities or as part of GVCs. Such support can involve technical assistance for innovation and the upscaling of local and traditional knowledge to promote climate resilience and adaptation as well as undertake mitigation activities.

Guidance notes, assessment tools and knowledge products must be prepared by gender advocates in domestic economy, at both national and subnational levels, regionally and globally, working with the gender focal points in the UNFCC as well as the GCF, trade ministries and export promotion agencies, in order to facilitate compliance with the integration of gender perspective in climate policy and the mandate from the Marrakech Meeting. This is already legitimised under the UNFCCC, as there is a mandate that invites parties to undertake and participate in the training and awareness building of both female and male delegates on issues related to gender balance and climate change; building the skills and capacity of their female delegates to participate effectively in the UNFCCC meetings; mainstreaming a gender perspective in the enhancement of climate technology development and transfer; integrating local and traditional knowledge in the formulation of climate policy; and recognising the value of the participation of grassroots women in gender-responsive climate actions at all levels (Decision 21/CP.22, paragraphs 7 and 24). A similar process needs to be developed for the trade area. This type of bottom-up process could conceivably be an outcome of the activities aimed at implementing the WTO Gender Declaration of 2017.

5.2.1 Adaptation and mitigation approach: linking to trade capacity and opportunity

Furthermore, policy-makers and climate and trade negotiators need to be informed by the findings of studies, with explicit policy implications, addressing the interplay between, on the one hand, adaptation and mitigation, trade development and promotion and, on the other hand, women's agency, their assets and resources, and their ability to access climate and trade finance, participate in mitigation projects and undertake sustainable adaptation. Grassroots women, researchers and gender machineries should become more involved in national adaptation and trade-related processes, both at the sector level and economy-wide. Climate funds such as the

GCF and the Adaptation funds that support adaptation and related processes have in-built mechanisms to facilitate the inclusion of women and gender perspectives in the proposal acceptance, approval and implementation stages of these activities. The adaptation process consists of four key components which will require the active participation of women, women's and community groups as part of multi-stakeholders' processes: (1) the assessment of climate impacts and vulnerability; (2) planning for adaptation; (3) the implementation of adaptation measures; and (4) the monitoring and evaluation of adaptation actions. Gender and trade aspects can play an important informative and useful role in all of these components, (UNFCCC 2014).

Moreover, ideally, some of the one-off US$3 million that the GCF has set aside for each country to support the adaptation-planning process could be accessed for education, training and public awareness that include trade components, especially in areas such as agriculture, food and nutrition, water, energy and health. The ongoing iterative adaptation-planning processes could detail ways to further embed the gender sensitisation and trade linkages in the investment and financing plans that are to be created under the NAPs process. Some of the trade aspects could also be funded through the Aid for Trade and trade-related capacity-building process at the sector level.

5.2.2 Gender and women's machineries: linking gender, climate, trade and sustainable development

Lastly, there is scope and need to build the capacities of national women's machineries at all levels on climate change and gender, trade and gender equality, women's empowerment and their interlinkages. As key stakeholders, these entities need to understand better so that they can engage more constructively with adaptation planning and its links to sectors that are important for women and add much value to exporting and enhancing women's income and the market share of SMEs (including smallholder farmers). Gender machineries must also have their capacity built to participate in the reviews of NDCs (expected to occur every five years), national export strategies, overall development and climate change planning, including the setting in place and implementation of energy and economic diversification strategies. Building on and enhancing the experiences with gender-responsive planning and budget processes, capacity-building workshops can also explore the fiscal expenditure linkages with climate change adaptation and mitigation actions and trade, as well as promoting access to, and the efficient and effective utilisation of, climate and trade finance to empower women and promote gender equality. This can be achieved by setting in place processes and mechanisms to ensure that climate change adaptation and mitigation policies, programmes and strategies aim to support the elimination of historical and structural gender biases, discrimination and other social constraints and promote women's, girls', boys' and men's wellbeing.

UN Women, with the close support and guidance of the GCF, has recently released a guidebook, *Leveraging Co-benefits between Gender Equality and Climate Action for Sustainable Development* (2016). That and Williams (2015), *Gender and Climate Finance: Coming Out of the Margin* could be useful contributions to this endeavour.

In the trade area, the Commonwealth Secretariat's set of publications on gender and trade could be updated to take into account new areas such as trade facilitation, government procurement agreement, GVCs and e-commerce in the context of climate–trade linkages, as useful tools to help both gender ministries, trade ministries, the private sector and NGOs better link trade and gender issues to policies, projects and programmes in Commonwealth countries.

5.2.3 Furthering research on gender and trade and integrating gender and climate issues

In both the trade and gender and climate and gender spheres, there is a need for greater and more rigorous evidence building for proactive policy advocacy and awareness raising of political and economic decision-makers. Underlying all of this is the need for data generation within and across countries, including gender-disaggregated data, which is also a pervasive challenge in SDG target 17.18.[6] However, it is important to recognise that data alone is insufficient to affect the problems of gender inequality and lack of women's empowerment that underlie and are increasingly exacerbated by trade policies and rules making as well as the climate change crisis and approaches adopted to resolve it. Data generation and gathering, thus must be grounded in framework that includes thorough awareness and accounting for the pervading global and regional structural inequalities in development dynamics that underlying women's social and economic situation in developing countries.

Hence, a strong focus of policy-oriented research on the gender–climate–trade nexus must also factor in the gender and social dimensions of global macroeconomic issues such as sovereign indebtedness, monetary and fiscal policies, tax avoidance (particularly so-called 'strategic transfer pricing') and evasion by corporations. These features of the global economy work to divert and distort domestic financial resources that could go to infrastructure and address natural disasters that could make women's lives and work in trade and non-trade sector better.

This analysis should complement the increased use of gender-sensitive tracking indicators (that are both common and comparable) and the collection and evaluation of data for trade and climate indicators. This could also be part of capacity-building, knowledge-sharing and ongoing learning processes.

As noted by Ratna (2010a), with regard to gender and trade issues in India (and elsewhere), there is a lack of consistent and validated data – about individual industries, about MSMEs and about female ownership of companies throughout the economy, using census data or sample surveys. Obviously, an important starting point is the identification of sectors that are currently dominated by women employees and women business owners and targeting support to those. Also in negotiating trade agreements there needs to be sensitivity about defensive interests (products and employment).

In addition, on the trade front, as with climate change finance, there are multiple instruments and mechanisms to help support countries to integrate the gender perspective and women's empowerment concerns into trade policy-making at national, regional and multilateral levels. For example, as noted earlier, better and more proactive use could be made of Aid for Trade and trade-related capacity-building initiatives such as the Standards and Trade Development Facility (STDF) and the Enhanced Integrated Framework.[7]

Discussions which focus attention on threshold issues such as the financial, time and physical resource costs of adapting to climate change that are incurred by particular groups of women (e.g. agricultural food producers and fishers) would greatly enrich understanding of how these elements interlink. A framework for assessing trade against gender and climate risk can be used to make these costs more visible. This can help to provide the basis for securing funding for gender equality objectives and women's economic empowerment in the context of the emerging climate change financing architecture, and mega and plurilateral trade agreement trends. There is a need for broad-spectrum and comprehensive research, and for capacity-building programming aimed at stimulating the development of tools and methodologies for further identification of women-specific climate-related trade opportunities, challenges and vulnerabilities. For example, there is need for much more work on:

- *Cross-regional comparisons in term of six specific areas:* nutrient capacity and women's health; social reproduction, social care and women's domestic burden and increased hardships; women's reduced ability to protect themselves; religious and social dogma concerns; lack of education; and unequal power relations. The opportunities, challenges and constraints face women-owned/operated MSMEs as independent entities as well as those integrated into global supply chains. Undergirding these comparisons must be:

    – gender audits of vulnerability, methodologies of climate change assessment, and ex ante and ex post gender audits of trade policy, agreements and reform agendas;

    – programmes and projects to reduce women's and girls' vulnerability to climate change effects and to enhance their ability to expand livelihood opportunities across the domestic economy and trade sectors.

- *Gender climate-trade interlinked sectoral issues:* agriculture (food security, adaptation); water, health, sanitation and livelihood; clean energy, energy efficiency and renewable energy – all with an awareness of the issues of traditional knowledge and constraints around women and intellectual property rights. Gender, climate change adaptation and informal economies also come under this heading.

Issues that offer good thematic intersectionality include:

- Climate-change-induced sectoral reallocation of production and its trade and gender impacts. Key questions could include: What production factors are reallocated from import-competing sectors toward exporting sectors when climate change induces extreme events with rapid onset (hurricanes, typhoons) or slow onset[8] (sea level rise and ocean acidification), with implications for, say, the tourism sector, and women's health sexual health and reproductive health? What are the magnitude and direction of sectoral labour reallocation in response to losses and damages (sustained) and consequent rehabilitation and/or any attempts at trade reform including trade liberalisation? What is the gender sensitivity and proactive actions around the reallocation of labour and resources across sectors? What is the impact on the sectoral pattern of trade? What are women's and men's capacities to undertake the necessary economic and social adjustments? What kinds of capacity-building support are needed?

- Closing knowledge gaps. The starting point for gender and trade is clear, exploring where the missing components and/or new directions are in trade policy-making. This may call for making useful and remedially oriented distinctions between the needs and capacities of LDCs, LLDCs, SIDS and middle-income countries in terms of dependency on factors such as cheap labour, agriculture, mining etc. that are vulnerable to climate variability.

5.2.4 Missing components

Components that are most prominently missing from gender and trade work were highlighted by Montes (2016) at a 2016 UNCTAD expert group meeting. These include the link between the degree of and the constraints around developing countries' policy space (e.g. to regulate private capital flows) to implement measures to propel their economies forward in order to address development gaps, including social and equity gaps.

Other areas that need to be at the forefront of the work on gender and trade, whether undertaken by UNCTAD or UN Women alone or in collaboration, such as with the Commonwealth Secretariat, include the integration of more explicit linkages of the transfer cost and adjustment burden of liberalisation-induced trade reforms on the household economy with men's and women's time use and unpaid labour, which is primarily impacting women's time poverty and other dimensions of economic poverty. It is also important, in this context, to explicitly link such issues with the lack of policy space, or the underutilisation of existing policy space, to promote gender equality and women's empowerment. Constraints on policy space may also spring from the regulatory and other untoward chill effects of Investor State Dispute Settlement (ISDS) provisions and the now pervasive use of ISDS cases against governments in developing countries,[9] as well as too restrictive rules on local content requirements and performance requirements in some trade and investment agreements.[10] These are not simply stand-alone issues, far removed from the conditions of the exercise of global macroeconomic, exchange rate and financial policy issues. Rather, they are very intimately interconnected, as not only may they exacerbate and perpetuate boom and bust cycles in the domestic economy but, more importantly from a gender perspective, they may inhibit progress on gender mainstreaming for women's empowerment and gender equality.

Another missing dimension of the work on gender and trade is the limited active and systematic participation of women's rights activism and critical feminist political economy approaches around the current issues on the trade agendas of both the WTO and the mega trade blocs discourse. This gap may be covered by the seeming rise and return of such activism with the formation of the Gender and Trade Coalition, which bills itself as a feminist alliance for trade justice. Should the coalition become as rigorous and active on both trade negotiation agenda and the implementation of trade policies as its antecedent, the International Gender and Trade Network (which faded during the 2008 financial crisis and the dormancy of the WTO trade liberalisation activities), then it will present a strong counter to any tendency to instrumentalize gender issues in the service of the forward momentum on unhampered trade liberalisation.

5.2.5 New directions

Future work needs to focus on the distinction between tradable goods and export orientation. Women are more involved in tradable foods, particularly in agriculture, including those sold on the domestic market, and not just export-oriented production. Much of the focus of current and past research has been on women as instruments in the export-oriented sector. This is most certainly the case for East Asia. However, in the current context, trade liberalisation in the manufacturing sector privileges large-scale manufacturing and may be disadvantageous to women (Montes 2016), though it can be argued that this can be offset by the integration of women workers and MSMEs into GVCs. However, the impact of GVCs on women's empowerment is not well researched. International businesses, which dominate these GVCs, may foster domestic regulations that may facilitate women's activities in these value chains. However, these may be precluded or severely restricted by investment and IPRs and by provisions in mega trade arrangements that go beyond the WTO TRIMs and TRIPS agreements (as well as investor suits clauses in bilateral investment treaties).

Trade policies that support gender equality and are sensitive to climate change require consistent and proactive interventions in order to make them strong instruments of women's economic and social empowerment. For example, on the trade side, among other support measures, women entrepreneurs, including small farmers, need support for a variety of purposes, including upgrading quality, reducing price (to compete with imports), organising to supply large volumes of exportable products and/or diversification into products for regional and global markets. Women's economic and social empowerment issues should also feature prominently in a renewed emphasis on areas such as GVCs, sanitary and phytosanitary issues, agriculture, domestic support, public stockholding, the Special Safeguard Mechanism and Special Safeguard Provision, export restrictions and fisheries subsidies. Careful rights-based gender analysis and gender impact assessments are warranted for emerging issue areas such as mega trade deals, domestic regulations on services, e-commerce/digital economy, MSMEs and investment facilitation.

A gender-responsive and strategic approach to trade policy and trade development (beyond the traditional absorption of cheap labour) may prove crucial for developing countries to benefit from trade and to unlock any significant and sustained dividends for poverty reduction and employment creation.

The discussion above points to the importance of the careful calibration of climate and trade policy to include the perspectives, voice and decision-making participation of women and men, taking into consideration their different challenges and constraints as well as the potential to take advantage of any emerging opportunities/dividends from such policies. In this regard, the building of capacity is an area for focused attention, and multiple strands of activity are developing for deepening capacity and enhancing the scientific and technical capacities of women and men.

Notes

1. This chapter draws freely on Williams (2019a,b).
2. The Commonwealth has four priority areas on gender equality: (1) women in leadership; (2) women's economic empowerment; (3) ending violence against women and girls; and (4) gender and climate change. It has a plethora of ongoing work on indicators for gender equality. In addition, the work on tracking on monitoring gender indicators and data development and management is spearheaded in some regions by various memoranda of understanding between different governments, international organisations such as the Commonwealth Secretariat or regional bodies such as CARICOM and UN Women.
3. The African Union has a central focus on achieving gender parity, and a gender scorecard has been developed to track progress made in achieving gender equality.
4. As part of its operational approach to helping to support developing countries to access the finance needed to implement climate actions under the UNFCCC agreed frameworks, the GCF offers a Readiness and Preparatory Support Programme, which consists of an offer of up to US$1 million per year per country, support to the national designated authority and a one-off US$3 million per country for the preparation of NAPs and related purposes. This is in addition to the country's access to the GCF funding for projects for country work programmes in mitigation and adaptation, as well as, the by local and international private sector through the GCF private sector window. The Fund is also committed to balance funding for adaptation and mitigation and to give special support to African, States, LDCs and small island developing states. Gender consideration is a core requirement of all GCF funded activities.
5. The Paris Committee on Capacity-building was established by the COP in 2015 as part of the adoption of the Paris Agreement to address gaps and needs, both current and emerging, in implementing capacity-building in developing-country Parties and further enhancing capacity-building efforts, including coherence and coordination in capacity-building activities under the Convention. Under its mandate, the committee is to take into consideration cross-cutting issues such as gender responsiveness, human rights and indigenous peoples' knowledge.
6. Target 17.18: 'By 2020, enhance capacity-building support to developing countries, including for least developed countries and small island developing States, to increase significantly the availability of high-quality, timely and reliable data disaggregated by income, gender, age, race, ethnicity, migratory status, disability, geographic location and other characteristics relevant in national contexts'.
7. The STDF supports developing countries in building their capacity to implement international sanitary and phytosanitary standards. The STDF has been noted to help women understand and implement sanitary and phytosanitary measures and thus to enter the supply chain in the flower sector in Uganda, and there is high hope that the STDF can help women, who are major players in the agricultural sector in developing countries. The Enhanced Integrated Framework promotes gender balance and inclusiveness in LDCs. It runs trade capacity programmes to support women's empowerment in Burkina Faso, Cambodia, Guinea, Mali, Nepal, Rwanda, Samoa, Solomon Islands and Vanuatu.
8. Though these events are gradual and may appear less destructive than rapid-onset extreme events, Matias (2017) notes that 'the UNFCCC found that the negative impacts of slow onset events are already affecting developing countries and there is an urgent need to manage the risks, despite the slow pace of the process.'

9   To date, there have been over 490 such cases against developing countries' governments by primarily foreign investors in reaction to changes in governmental regulations on issues such as environmental, health, mining rights and tax policies, to which investors take exception. Please see UNCTAD Investment Policy Hub (UNCTAD 2019.)
10 Performance requirements tend to be associated with investment agreements, whereas local content rules are more related to trade provisions.

Bibliography

Addis Ababa Action (2015) Addis Ababa Action Agenda of the Third International Conference on Financing for Development (Addis Ababa Action Agenda). The final text of the outcome document adopted at the Third International Conference on Financing for Development (Addis Ababa, Ethiopia, 13–16 July 2015) and endorsed by the General Assembly in its resolution 69/313 of 27 July 2015. United Nations New York, 2015.

African Development Bank (AfDB), Asian Development Bank, UK Department for International Development, European Commission Directorate-General for Development, German Federal Ministry for Economic Cooperation and Development, The Netherlands' Ministry of Foreign Affairs Development Cooperation, Organization for Economic Cooperation and Development, United Nations Development Programme (UNDP), United Nations Environmental Programme (UNEP), and The World Bank, 2003. 'Poverty and Climate Change - Reducing the Vulnerability of the Poor through Adaptation' World Bank: Washington, D.C.

Agarwal, B (2001), 'Common property institutions and sustainable governance of resources', *World Development*, Vol. **29**(10), 1649–72.

Aguayo-Tellez, E (2011), *The Impact of Trade Liberalization Policies and FDI on Gender Inequalities: A Literature Review*, WDR background paper, Washington, D.C.: World Bank.

Aguilar, L, M Granat and C Owren (2015), *Roots for the Future: The Landscape and Way Forward on Gender and Climate Change*, IUCN and GGCA, Washington, DC.

Aguilar, L., A. Quesada-Aguilar and D.M.P. Shaw (eds) (2011). Forests and Gender. Gland, Switzerland: IUCN and New York, NY: WEDO.

Aguirre, D, L Hoteit, C Rupp and K Sabbagh (2012), *Empowering the Third Billion: Women and the World of Work in 2012*, PricewaterhouseCoopers, available at: https://www.strategyand.pwc.com/media/file/Strategyand_Empowering-the-Third-Billion_Full-Report.pdf (accessed 13 June 2019).

Alston, M., K. L. Whittenbury, A. L. Haynes and N. J. Godden (2014). Are climate challenges reinforcing child and forced marriage and dowry as adaptation strategies in the context of Bangladesh? *Women's Studies International Forum*, **47**, 137–144. https://doi.org/10.1016/j.wsif.2014.08.005

Angelsen, A and L Jumbe (2007), 'Forest dependence and participation in CPR management: empirical evidence from forest co-management in Malawi', *Ecological Economics*, Vol. **62** (3-4), 661–72.

Antonopoulos, R (2009), *The Current Economic and Financial Crisis: A Gender Perspective*, Working Paper No. 562, Levy Economics Institute of Bard College, New York.

APEC (2018), '24th Meeting of APEC Ministers Responsible for Trade Statement', available at: https://www.apec.org/Meeting-Papers/Sectoral-Ministerial-Meetings/Trade/2018_trade (accessed 14 June 2019).

Arora-Jonsson, S (2011), 'Virtue and vulnerability: discourses on women, gender and climate change', *Global Environmental Change*, Vol. **21**, 744–51.

Atil, M. (2012), *Women & Business in South Sudan*, available at https://www.academia.edu/1242725/Women_and_Business_in_South_Sudan (accessed 05 September 2019).

Aucan, J (2018), Effects of Climate Change on Sea Levels and Inundation Relevant to the Pacific Islands. Pacific marine climate change report card', *Science Review 2018*, 43–49. https://reliefweb.int/sites/reliefweb.int/files/resources/4_Sea_Level_and_Inundation.pdf

Ba, K, M Thiaw, N Lazar, A Sarr, T Brochier, I Ndiaye et al. (2016), 'Resilience of key biological parameters of the Senegalese flat sardinella to overfishing and climate change', *PLoS ONE*, Vol. **11**(6), e0156143. doi: 10.1371/journal.pone.0156143.

Bandele, O (2015), An Equal Seat at the Table: Gendering Trade Policy, Trade Competitiveness Briefing Paper, the Commonwealth Secretariat. https://www.oecd-ilibrary.org/docserver/5jm0qglb1s9s-en.pdf?expires=1572448430&id=id&accname=guest&checksum=61F4C46385D7327FCD0F548D1CC1ECC7

Beatley, M (2018), 'Senegalese women turn to export fish in spite of local shortages', *Global Post*, available at: https://www.pri.org/stories/2018-03-30/senegalese-women-turn-exporting-fish-spite-local-shortages (accessed 11 June 2019).

Beatley, M and S Edwards (2018), 'Overfished: in Senegal, empty nets lead to hunger and violence', *Global Post Investigations*, available at https//:gpinvestigations.pri.org/overfished-in-senegal-empty-nets-lead-to-humger-and-violence-e3b5d0c9686 (accessed 13 June 2019).

Benavides, L (2018a), 'How climate change disproportionately harms Senegalese women', https://psmag.com/environment/how-climate-change-hurts-senegalese-women (accessed 13 June 2019).

Benavides, L (2018b), 'As Senegal's fish stocks collapse, women are more vulnerable than ever', available at: https://www.newsdeeply.com/womensadvancement/articles/2018/05/23/as-senegals-fish-stocks-collapse-women-are-more-vulnerable-than-ever (accessed 13 June 2019).

Bird, N, T Beloe, M Hedger, J Lee, K Nicholson, N O'Donnell, S Gooty, A Heikens, P Steele, A Mackay and M Miller (2012), *The Climate Public Expenditure and Institutional Review (CPEIR): A Methodology to Review Climate Policy, Institutions and Expenditure*, joint UNDP/ODI working paper, UNDP.

Birdsall, N., David Ross and Richard Sabot (1995). Inequality and Growth Reconsidered: Lessons from East Asia *the World Bank Economic Review* **Vol. 9**, No. 3 (Sep., 1995), pp. 477–508.

Blessings, C, L Jume and A Angelsen (2006), 'Do the poor benefit from devolution policies? Evidence from Malawi's Forest co-management program', *Land Economics*, Vol. **82**(4), 562–81.

Bloom, DE, M Kuhn and K Prettner (2017), 'Invest in women and prosper', *Finance & Development*, Vol. **54**, No. 3, p. 50–55.

Boyd, E (2002) 'The Noel Kempff Project in Bolivia: gender, power and decision making in climate mitigation', in Masika, R (Ed.), *Gender and Development* **Vol. 10**, No. 2, Climate Change (Jul., 2002), pp. 70–77. Taylor & Francis, Ltd. on behalf of Oxfam GB https://www.jstor.org/stable/4030576

BP Energy Outlook 2018 edition. BP plc, available https://www.bp.com/content/dam/bp/business-sites/en/global/corporate/pdfs/energy-economics/energy-outlook/bp-energy-outlook-2018.pdf (accessed 7 August 2019).

BRIDGE (2008), *Gender and Climate Change: Mapping the Linkages. A Scoping Study on Knowledge and Gaps*, Brighton: Institute of Development Studies, University of Sussex, Sussex.

BRIDGE (2016), *Gender and Climate Change*, Brighton: Institute for Development Studies, University of Sussex, Sussex.

Brides of the sun (2016), 'An investigation into how climate change is creating a generation of child brides', available at: https://www.bridesofthesun.com (accessed 13 June 2019).

Bussolo, M and RE De Hoyos (2009), *Gender Aspects of the Trade and Poverty Nexus: A Macro-Micro Approach*, World Bank, Washington, DC.

Cagatay, N (2001), *Trade, Gender, and Poverty*, UNDP, New York.

Care (2016), *Hope Dries Up? Women and Girls Coping with Drought and Climate Change in Mozambique*, Maputo: Care International Mozambique.

Carr, M and M Williams (2010), *Trading Stories: Experiences with Gender and Trade*, Commonwealth Secretariat, London.

Chamberlain, G. (2017), Why climate change is creating a new generation of child brides https://www.theguardian.com/society/2017/nov/26/climate-change-creating-generation-of-child-brides-in-africa

Convention on Biological Diversity (2018) Mobilisation of Trade: Doha negotiations related to biodiversity, WTO Agreements and biodiversity measures, trade in sustainable development. https://www.cbd.int/financial/0035.shtml (accessed 2 August 2019).

CCAP (n.d.), 'Pakistan distributed generation from renewable energy (DG RE) NAMA', available at: http://ccap.org/pakistan-distributed-generation-from-renewable-energy-dg-re-nama-project/ (accessed 13 June 2019).

CDKN (2017), 'Driving, connecting and communicating the many roles of national government in climate change adaptation planning', Climate & Development Knowledge Network.

CEDAW (2009), Statement of the CEDAW Committee on Gender and Climate Change, Committee on Gender and Climate Change, CEDAW 44th Session, August 2009.

CEDAW (2018), General Recommendation No. 37 on gender-related dimensions of disaster risk reduction in the context of climate change, Committee on the Elimination of Discrimination against Women, CEDAW/C/GC/37.

Chamberlain, G (2017), 'Why climate change is creating a new generation of child brides', *The Guardian*, 26 November, available at: https://www.theguardian.com/society/2017/nov/26/climate-change-creating-generation-of-child-brides-in-africa (accessed 14 June 2019).

Cheung, WW, R Watson and D Pauly (2013), 'Signature of ocean warming in global fisheries catch', *Nature*, Vol. **497**, 365–368.

CIDA (2009), 'Gender equality and climate change: why consider gender equality when taking action on climate change?' Quebec: Canadian International Development Agency. https://www.oecd.org/dac/gender-development/44896501.pdf (accessed 05 September 2019).

CIFOR (2013), *Gender in the CGIAR Research Program on Forests, Trees and Agroforestry: A Strategy for Research and Action*, Center for International Forestry Research (CIFOR), Bogor, Indonesia.

CIFs (2010), *Strategic Environment, Social and Gender Assessment of the Climate Investment Funds*, SCF/TFC.6/Inf.2. https://www.climateinvestmentfunds.org/sites/cif_enc/files/meeting-documents/ctf_inf_3_env_soc_gender_assessment_nov_2010_0.pdf (accessed 05 September 2019).

CIFs (2013). Gender Review of CIF. Prepared by Global Gender Office of the International Union for Conservation of Nature – IUCN. Lorena Aguilar, Francois Rogers, Rebecca Pearl-Martinez, Itza Castaneda, Andrea Athanas and Jackeline Siles. https://www.climateinvestmentfunds.org/sites/cif_enc/files/CIF_GENDER_REVIEW_FINAL_March_11.pdf (accessed 05 September 2019).

Climate Strategies (2018), *Policy Brief: Making Trade Work for Climate, Options for Policymakers*, available at: https://climatestrategies.org/publication/pb-trade-options-for-policymakers/ (accessed 13 June 2019).

CMW, CEDAW, UN Women and OHCHR (2016), 'Addressing gender dimensions in large-scale movements of migrants and refugees', available at: http://www.ohchr.org/EN/NewsEvents/Pages/DisplayNews.aspx?NewsID=20521&LangID=E (accessed 13 June 2019).

Coastal Resources Center (n.d.), 'USAID/COMFISH and USAID/COMFISH PLUS: collaborative management for a sustainable fisheries future in Senegal', available at: https://www.crc.uri.edu/stories_page/bridging-the-gender-and-cultural-gap-in-senegals-fisheries-sector/ (accessed 10 June 2019).

Coche, I., B. Kotschwar and J. M. Salazar-Xirinachs (2006), *Gender Issues in Trade Policy-Making*, Organization of the American States Department of Trade, Tourism and Competitiveness Executive Secretariat for Integral Development (SEDI), Washington, DC.

COMFISH/USAID (2012), *Annual Report October 2011–September 2012: USAID/COMFISH Project PENCOO GEJ Collaborative Management for a Sustainable Fisheries Future in Senegal*, Dakar, Senegal: USAID.

Commission on the Status of Women (2016), *Women's Empowerment and the Link to Sustainable Development: Agreed Conclusions* (advanced unedited version), 60th session, 14–24 March 2016, UN Commission on the Status of Women.

Commission on the Status of Women (various dates), Resolutions on 'Gender equality and the empowerment of women in natural disaster', adopted by consensus at the 56th and 58th Sessions in March 2012 https://www.preventionweb.net/english/professional/policies/v.php?id=26388 (accessed 05 September 2019).

Dankelman, I (2002), 'Climate change: learning from gender analysis and women's experience of organizing for sustainable development', in Masika, R (Ed.), *Gender, Development and Climate Change*, Oxfam Publishing, Oxford.

Dankelman, I (Ed.) (2010), *Gender and Climate Change: An Introduction*, EarthScan, London.

De Melo, J and NA Mathys (2010), *Trade and Climate Change: The Challenges Ahead*, FERDI, Paris.

Derboghossian, A (2018), 'Making Aid for Trade work for women', *International Trade Forum*, **Vol. 1**, 24–25, available at: http://www.intracen.org/uploadedFiles/

Common/Content/TradeForum/Trade_Forum_1_2018.pdf (accessed 13 June 2019).

De Silva, DAM (2011), *Faces of Women in Global Fishery Value Chains: Female Involvement, Impact and Importance in the Fisheries of Developed and Developing Countries*, NORAD/FAO Value Chain Project, available at: http://www.google.com/url?sa=t&rct=j&q=&esrc=s&source=web&cd=1&ved=2ahUKEwjOq8as9 MXhAhVKLFAKHeQrDWUQFjAAegQIAxAC&url=http%3A%2F%2Fwww.fao.org%2Ffileadmin%2Fuser_upload%2Ffisheries%2Fdocs%2FThe_role_of_Women_in_the_fishery_value_chain_Dr__De_Silva.doc&usg=AOvVaw3Fn8X LEVIRveL0X40YPddl (accessed 14 June 2019).

Dey, J (1981), 'Gambian women: unequal partners in rice development projects?', *Journal of Development Studies*, Vol. 17(3), 109–122. https://www.tandfonline.com/doi/abs/10.1080/00220388108421801 (accessed 7 August 2019).

DIHK (Deutscher Industrie- und Handelskammertag) (2018), 'Idea paper: WTO SME initiative now!', available at: https://www.politico.eu/wp-content/uploads/2018/10/DIHK_WTO-Mittelstandsinitiative-umsetzen_01.10.2018_EN.pdf (accessed 13 June 2019).

Dunn, L, A Hamilton, J Byron and Q Palmer (2009), *Gender and Women's Rights Analysis of Economic Partnership Agreements: The Implementation of Trade Liberalisation Jamaica*. https://www.empowerwomen.org/-/media/files/un%20women/knowledge%20gateway/resourcefiles/2014/04/21/18/27/gender-trade-and-epa-jamaica_research.pdf (accessed 05 September 2019).

ECOWAS and ITC (n.d.), *Strategic Orientation Document for Mango Value Chain in the Economic Community of West African States (ECOWAS)*, Abjua: ECOWAS/ITC.

ECOWAS Centre for Renewable Energy and Energy Efficiency (ECREE) (2015), *Situation Analysis of Energy and Gender Issues in ECOWAS Member States 2015: The ECOWAS Policy for Gender Mainstreaming in Energy Access*, ECOWAS, Abuja.

ECOWAS Commission (2013), *Final Report on Gender and Trade Workshop*, ECOWAS, Abuja.

Eggerts, E and JA Gari (2017), *Forests and Gender: A Catalytic Alliance for Sustainable Development*, International Institute for Sustainable Development. Winnipeg, Canada: IISD.

Elson, D (2010), 'Gender and the global economic crisis in developing countries: a framework for analysis', *Gender and Development*, Vol. 18, 201–12.

Equations (2000), *Continuing Saga of Marginalisation: A Dossier on Women and Tourism*. New Thippasandra, Bangalore: EQUATIONS Equitable Tourism Options. https://www.equitabletourism.org/files/fileDocuments790_uid13.pdf (accessed 05 September 2019).

Equations (2001), *Trade in Tourism through the GATS: Interests of Developing Countries at Stake*. New Thippasandra, Bangalore: EQUATIONS Equitable Tourism Options.

Etizinger, A, K Rhiney, S Caromna, I van Loosen and M Taylor (2015), *Jamaica: Assessing the Impact of Climate Change on Cocoa and Tomato*, CIAT Policy Brief No. 28, Centro Internacional de Agricultura Tropical, Cali, Columption.

European Commission (2018), Report from the Commission to the European Parliament, the Council, the European Economic and Social Committee and the Committee of the Regions on Implementation of Free Trade Agreements. COM (2018).

European Parliament (2011), Report on women and climate change (2011/2197(INI)), Committee on Women's Rights and Gender Equality, rapporteur Nicole Kiil-Nielsen, European Parliament.

European Institute for Gender Equality (2012), Review of the Implementation in the EU of Area K of the Beijing Platform for Action: Women and the Environment. Gender Equality and Climate Change. https://genderandenvironment.org/resource/review-of-the-implementation-in-the-eu-of-area-k-of-the-beijing-platform-for-action-women-and-the-environment-gender-equality-and-climate-change/ (accessed 05 September 2019).

FAO (1999a). Non-wood Forest Products. Forestry Information Notes. Rome.

FAO, http://www.fao.org.

FAO (1999B). State of the World's Forests 1999. Rome: FAO, http://www.fao.org.

FAO (2008), EAF–Nansen Project Report No. 5, EAF-N/PR/5, Annual forum of the EAF-Nansen project, Theme: the ecosystem approach to fisheries, Opportunities for Africa, FAO, Rome.

FAO (2009), Rural Women and the Right to Food, FAO, Rome.

FAO (2011), The State of Food and Agriculture 2010-2011. Women in Agriculture, Closing the Gender Gap in Agriculture. FAO, Rome. http://www.fao.org/3/a-i2050e.pdf (accessed 05 September 2019).

FAO (2012a), The State of World Fisheries and Aquaculture 2012, FAO, Rome.

FAO (2012b), Report of the FAO Workshop on Future Direction of Gender and Aquaculture and Fisheries: Action, Research and Development. FAO Fisheries and Aquaculture Report No. 998 FIRA/R998 (En). Rome: FAO

FAO (2014), The State of World Fisheries and Aquaculture: Opportunities and Challenges 2014. Rome: FAO. http://www.fao.org/3/a-i3720e.pdf (accessed 05 September 2019).

FAO (2016), The State of Food and Agriculture: Climate Change, Agriculture and Food Security, FAO, Rome. http://www.fao.org/3/a-i6030e.pdf (accessed 05 September 2019).

FAO (2016), Fisheries and Aquaculture and Climate Change, Rome: FAO. http://www.fao.org/3/a-i6383e.pdf (accessed 05 September 2019).

FAO (2018), Country Gender Assessment Series: National Gender Profile of Agriculture and Rural Livelihoods. Ghana, Rome: FAO.

Field, CB, V Barros, TF Stocker, D Qin, DJ Dokken, KL Ebi, MD Mastrandrea, KJ Mach, G-K Plattner, SK Allen, M Tignor and PM Midgley (Eds.) (2012), *Managing the Risks of Extreme Events and Disasters to Advance Climate Change Adaptation: A Special Report of Working Groups I and II of the Intergovernmental Panel on Climate Change*, Cambridge University Press, Cambridge.

Fontana, M (2007), 'Modelling the effects of trade on women, at work and at home: comparative perspectives', in Elson, D, C Grown and I Van Steveren (Eds.), *Feminist Economics of Trade*, Routledge, London.

Fontana, M (2009), *Gender Justice in Trade Policy: The Gender Effects of Economic Partnership Agreements*, One World Action, London.

Frohmann, A (2017), *Gender Equality and Trade Policy*, Working Paper No. 24/2017 December 2017 World Trade Institute and University of Bern.

Gaddis, I and J Pieters (2017), 'The gendered labor market impacts of trade liberalization: evidence from Brazil', *Journal of Human Resources*, Vol. **52**(2), 457–90.

Gammage, S, C Manfre and K Cook (2009), *Gender and Pro-Poor Value Chain Analysis: Insights from the Gate Project Methodology and Case Studies*, USAID, available at: https://pdfs.semanticscholar.org/0dc6/aa3aaf2196616c94eb6a722b456afd4bb103.pdf (accessed 14 June 2019).

GDPRD (2010), *Gender and Agriculture*, Platform Policy Brief No. 3, Global Donor Platform for Rural Development, Bonn.

GEF (2015), 'Workshop looks at gender, climate change and monitoring & evaluation issues in sanitation management', available at: https://www.gefcrew.org/images/announcements/GEFCReW_MediaAnnouncement_Governance_Sanitation_Workshop_Antigua_Feb2015_Final.pdf. https://www.caribank.org/news/workshop-looks-at-gender-climate-change-and-monitoring-evaluation-issues-in-sanitation-management.

Gennovate (2018), *Challenging Gender Myths: Promoting Inclusive Wheat and Maize Research for Development in Nepal*, available at: https://gennovate.org/wp-content/uploads/2018/10/Challenging_gender_myths_Nepal_Gennovate_Tool.pdf (accessed 14 June 2019).

GFC (2009), *The Hottest REDD Issues: Rights, Equity, Development, Deforestation and Governance by Indigenous Peoples and Local Communities*, Commission on Environmental, Economic and Social Policy and Global Forest Coalition. https://wrm.org.uy/wp-content/uploads/2013/05/Hottest_REDD_issues.pdf (Accessed 05 September 2019).

GFC (2008) Global Forest Coalition, "Life as Commerce, the impact of market-based conservation on Indigenous Peoples, local communities and women", http://www.globalforestcoalition.org/wp-content/uploads/2010/12/Impacts-marketbasedconservationmechanisms-on-woman4.pdf

GGCA and UNDP (2011), *Gender and Climate Finance*, UNDP, New York.

Gholizadeh Nojehdeh, H (2017), *Fishery Sector in the WTO and UNFCCC: Outlining a Synergetic Approach*, CUTS International, Geneva.

GIVRAPD (2014a), 'Jamaica profile', Global Islands' Vulnerability Research Adaptation Policy and Development, Global Islands' Vulnerability Research Adaptation Policy Development (GIVRAPD) project. Christ Church.

GIVRAPD (2014b), 'Saint Lucia profile', Global Islands' Vulnerability Research Adaptation Policy and Development, Christ Church. Global Islands' Vulnerability Research Adaptation Policy Development (GIVRAPD) project. Christ Church.

Government of Barbados (2015), Barbados Intended Nationally Determined Contribution, https://www4.unfccc.int/sites/ndcstaging/PublishedDocuments/Barbados%20First/Barbados%20INDC%20FINAL%20September%20%2028,%202015.pdf

Government of Canada (2018), 'Highlighting gender in trade', available at: http://international.gc.ca/gac-amc/publications/blueprint_2020-objectif_2020/highlighting_gender_trade-mettre_accent_sur_genre_commerce.aspx?lang=eng (accessed 12 June 2019).

Government of India (2015), India's Intended Nationally Determined Contribution: Working towards climate justice. https://www4.unfccc.int/sites/ndcstaging/PublishedDocuments/India%20First/INDIA%20INDC%20TO%20UNFCCC.pdf

Government of Kenya (2015), Kenya's Intended Nationally Determined Contribution (INDC) Ministry of Environment and Natural Resources. https://www4.unfccc.int/sites/submissions/INDC/Published%20Documents/Kenya/1/Kenya_INDC_20150723.pdf

Government of Nigeria (2015) Nigeria's Intended Nationally Determined Contributionhttps://www4.unfccc.int/sites/NDCStaging/Pages/Search.aspx?k=Nigeria

Government of Singapore (2015), Singapore's Intended Nationally Determined Contribution (Indc) and Accompanying Information https://www4.unfccc.int/sites/ndcstaging/PublishedDocuments/Singapore%20First/Singapore%20INDC.pdf

Government Sri Lanka (2015), Nationally Determined Contributions https://www4.unfccc.int/sites/ndcstaging/PublishedDocuments/Sri%20Lanka%20First/NDCs%20of%20Sri%20Lanka.pdf

Government of South Africa (2015), South Africa's Intended Nationally Determined Contribution (INDC). https://www4.unfccc.int/sites/submissions/INDC/Published%20Documents/South%20Africa/1/South%20Africa.pdf

Government of Zambia (2015), Zambia's intended nationally determined contribution (indc) to the 2015 agreement on climate change https://www4.unfccc.int/sites/ndcstaging/PublishedDocuments/Zambia First/FINAL+ZAMBIA'S+INDC_1.pdf

Hansen, J, P Kharecha, M Sato, V Masson-Delmotte, F Ackerman, DJ Beerling, PJ Hearty, O Hoegh-Guldberg, S-L Hsu and C Parmesan (2013), 'Assessing "dangerous climate change": required reduction of carbon emissions to protect young people, future generations and nature', *PloS ONE*, **Vol. 8**, e.0081648, available at https://doi.org/10.1371/journal.pone.0081648 (accessed 14 June 2019).

Harrington, R (2016), 'These 10 countries are ramping up clean energy more than any others', *Business Insider*, available at: http://uk.businessinsider.com/top-renewable-energy-investments-by-country-2016-3?r=US&IR=T/#10-chile-34 (accessed 14 June 2019).

Higgins, K (2012), *Gender Dimensions of Trade Facilitation and Logistics: A Guidance Note*, World Bank, Washington, DC.

Higgins, K (2013), *Gender and Free Trade Agreements: Best Practices and Policy Guidance*, North-South Institute, available at: http://www.nsi-ins.ca/wp-content/uploads/2013/03/2013-Gender-and-FTAs-Best-Practices-and-Policy-Guidance.pdf (accessed 14 June 2019).

Hoddinott, J and L Haddad (1995), 'Does female income share influence household expenditures? Evidence from Côte d'Ivoire', *Oxford Bulletin of Economics and Statistics*, Vol. **57**(1), 77–96.

Howse, R (2010), *Climate Mitigation Subsidies and the WTO Legal Framework: A Policy Analysis*, International Institute for Sustainable Development, available at: https://www.iisd.org/pdf/2009/bali_2_copenhagen_subsidies_legal.pdf (accessed 14 June 2019).

Hufbauer, GC, S Charnovitz and J Kim (2009), *Global Warming and the World Trading System*, Peterson Institute for International Economics, Washington, DC.

Hunt, J, S Lateef and HT Thomas (2007), *Gender Action Plans and Gender Equality Results: Rapid Gender Assessments of the ADB Projects Synthesis Report*, Asian Development Bank, Gender, Social Development, and Civil Society Division.

IEA (2017), *Tracking Clean Energy Innovation Progress*, International Energy Agency, Paris, available at:https://www.iea.org/media/etp/tracking2017/TrackingCleanEnergyInnovationProgress.pdf (accessed 14 June 2019).

IEA (2018), *World Energy Outlook 2018, Executive Summary*, International Energy Agency, Paris, available at: https://webstore.iea.org/download/summary/190?fileName=English-WEO-2018-ES.pdf (accessed 7 August 2019).

ILO (2015), *SME and Decent Productive Employment Creation*, prepared for G-20, ILO, Geneva.

ILO (2016), *Women at Work: Trends 2016*, International Labour Office, Geneva.

IMF (2016), *She Is the Answer*, Finance and Development, March 2016, **Vol.53**, No.1

IMF (2018a), *World Economic Output October 2018*, IMF, Washington, DC.

IMF (2018b), *Pursuing Women's Economic Empowerment*, IMF, Washington, DC.

IMF, World Bank and WTO (2017), *Making Trade an Engine of Growth for All*, IMF, Washington, DC.

International Trade Centre (2017), *SheTrades: Promoting SME Competitiveness in Indonesia*. ITC, Geneva.

Halsnaes, K. et al. (2007) Framing Issues in Climate Change 2007: Mitigation. Contribution of Working Group III to the Fourth Assessment Report of the Intergovernmental Panel on Climate Change. [Metz, B., O. R. Davidson, P. R. Bosch, R. Dave and L. A. Meyer (eds)], Cambridge University Press, Cambridge, United Kingdom and New York, NY, USA. Chapter 2.1.3, pg. 121. The dual relationship between climate change and Sustainable Development. Working Group III: Mitigation of Climate Change. IPCC (2007). https://www.ipcc.ch/site/assets/uploads/2018/02/ar4-wg3-chapter2-1.pdf [accessed 6 August 2019].

ICIMOD (2009), 'Engendering Agriculture on Unequal Terms in the Hindu Kush-Himilayas: Case Studies from Nepal and India'. International Center for Integrated Mountain Development, Kathmandu, Nepal. Cited in Nellemann et al 2011. http://www.zaragoza.es/contenidos/medioambiente/onu/1207-eng.pdf (accessed 6 August 2019).

IPCC (2013), 'Summary for policymakers', in Stocker, TF, D Qin, G-K Plattner, M Tignor, SK Allen, J Boschung, A Nauels, Y Xia, V Bex and PM Midgley (Eds.), *Climate Change 2013: The Physical Science Basis. Contribution of Working Group I to the Fifth Assessment Report of the Intergovernmental Panel on Climate Change*, Cambridge University Press, Cambridge.

IPCC, 2013. Summary for Policymakers. In: Climate Change 2013: The Physical Science Basis. Contribution of Working Group I to the Fifth Assessment Report of the Intergovernmental Panel on Climate Change [Stocker, T.F., D. Qin, G.-K. Plattner, M. Tignor, S.K. Allen, J. Boschung, A. Nauels, Y. Xia, V. Bex and P.M. Midgley (eds.)]. Cambridge University Press, Cambridge, United Kingdom and New York, NY, USA.

IPCC, 2014a: *Climate Change 2014: Impacts, Adaptation, and Vulnerability. Part A: Global and Sectoral Aspects. Contribution of Working Group II to the Fifth Assessment Report of the Intergovernmental Panel on Climate Change* [Field, C.B., V.R. Barros, D.J. Dokken, K.J. Mach, M.D. Mastrandrea, T.E. Bilir, M. Chatterjee, K.L. Ebi, Y.O. Estrada, R.C. Genova, B. Girma, E.S. Kissel, A.N. Levy, S. MacCracken, P.R. Mastrandrea, and L.L. White (eds.)]. Cambridge University Press, Cambridge, United Kingdom and New York, NY, USA, 1132 pp.

IPCC, 2014b: *Climate Change 2014: Impacts, Adaptation, and Vulnerability. Part B: Regional Aspects. Contribution of Working Group II to the Fifth Assessment Report of the Intergovernmental Panel on Climate Change* [Barros, V.R., C.B. Field, D.J. Dokken, M.D. Mastrandrea, K.J. Mach, T.E. Bilir, M. Chatterjee, K.L. Ebi, Y.O. Estrada, R.C. Genova, B. Girma, E.S. Kissel, A.N. Levy, S. MacCracken, P.R. Mastrandrea and L.L. White (eds.)]. Cambridge University Press, Cambridge, United Kingdom and New York, NY, USA, 688 pp.

IUCN, UNDP and Global Gender and Climate Alliance (2010), *Training Manual on Gender and Climate Change*, IUCN, UNDP, Global Gender and Climate Alliance (GGCA).

Jackson, J and J Wedderburn (2009), *Gender and the Economic Partnership Agreement: An Analysis of the Potential Gender Effects of the CARIFORUM-EU EPA*, Caribbean Development Report 2, pp. 123-203, available at: http://www.cepal.org/publicaciones/xml/3/38253/LCARL.245part3.pdf (accessed 14 August 2017).

Jaeger, CC and J Jaeger (2011), 'Three views of two degrees', *Regional Environmental Change*, Vol. 11 (Suppl. 1), S15–S26, doi: 10.1007/s10113-010-0190-9.

Jerneck, A (2017), 'Taking gender seriously in climate change adaptation and sustainability science research: views from feminist debates and sub-Saharan small-scale agriculture', *Sustainability Science*, Vol. **13**(2), 103–16. doi: 10.1007/s11625-017-0464-y.

Kabeer, N (2003), *Gender Mainstreaming in Poverty Eradication and the Millennium Development Goals*, London: Commonwealth Secretariat.

Khalfani, FS (2015), 'The agro-food industry measurement', paper presented at the FAO-UNIDO Expert Group Meeting, Rome, 23–24 November.

Khor, M (2010), *The Climate and Trade Relation: Some Issues*, Research Paper 29, South Centre, Geneva.

Khor, M, MF Montes, M Williams and VPB Yu III (2017), *Promoting Sustainable Development by Addressing the Impacts of Climate Change Response Measures on Developing Countries*, Research Paper 81. Geneva: South Centre.

Kinoshita, Y. and K. Kochhar (2016), She Is The Answer. Finance & Development, March 2016, **Vol. 53**, No. 1, https://www.imf.org/external/pubs/ft/fandd/2016/03/kinoshita.htm

Kis-Katos, K and R Sparrow (2015), 'Poverty, labor markets and trade liberalization in Indonesia', *Journal of Development Economics*, Vol. **117**, 94–106.

Klasen, S. (2002), Low Schooling for girls, slower growth for all? Cross-country evidence on the impact of gender inequality on development. World Bank Economic Review **vol.16**, no3, 345-373.

Korinek, J (2005), *Trade and Gender: Issues and Interactions*, OECD Trade Policy Working Paper No. 24, OECD, Paris.

Kwan, B (2017), 'The modern (fisher)woman: considering gender in fisheries', available at: https://nereusprogram.org/works/the-modern-fisherwoman-considering-gender-in-fisheries/ (accessed 14 June 2019).

Lambeth, L, B Hanchard, H Aslin, L Fay-Sauni, P Tuara, K Des Rochers and A Vunisea (2014), 'An overview of the involvement of women in fisheries activities in Oceania', *SPC Women in Fisheries Information Bulletin*, **25**, 21–33.

Ledrans, M, P Pirard, H Tillaut, M Pascal, S Vandentorren, F Suzan, G Salines, A Le Tertre, S Medina, A Maulpoix, B Bérat, N Carré, C Ermanel, H Isnard, C Ravault and MC Delmas (2004), 'The heat wave of August 2003: what happened?', *Revue du Praticien*, Vol. **54**(12), 1289–97.

Levinsohn, J (1999), 'Employment responses to international liberalization in Chile', *Journal of International Economics*, Vol. **47**(2), 321–44.

Locke, C (1999), 'Constructing a gender policy for joint forest management in India', *Development and Change*, Vol. **30**(2), 265–85.

Liu, J and D Goldstein (2013), 'Understanding China's renewable energy technology exports', *Energy Policy*, **Vol. 52**, 417–28, available at: https://doi.org/10.1016/j.enpol.2012.09.054 (accessed 14 June 2019).

LMS (2017) Lesotho's Nationally Determined Contribution under the United Nations Framework Convention. Ministry of Energy and Meterology, Lesotho.

Loo, Y. Y., L. Billa and A. Singh (2015), Effect of climate change on seasonal monsoon in Asia and its impact on the variability of monsoon rainfall in Southeast Asia. Geoscience Frontiers Volume 6, Issue 6, November 2015, Pages 817–823.

Maathai, W (2003), *Unbowed: The Green Belt Movement. Sharing the Approach and the Experience*, Lantern Books, New York.

MacDonald, R (2005), 'How women were affected by the tsunami: a perspective from Oxfam', *PLoS Med*, Vol. **2**(6), e178, available at: https://doi.org/10.1371/journal.pmed.0020178 (accessed 14 June 2019).

Maimbo, Samuel; Saranga, Tania; Strychacz, Nicholas. 2010. *Facilitating cross-border mobile banking in Southern Africa (English)*. Africa trade policy notes; no. 1. Washington, DC: World Bank.

Martinez, B (2013), 'Remunicipalisation in the water sector: an unstoppable wave. Notes on the debate and action', available at: https://www.tni.org/en/article/remunicipalisation-in-the-water-sector-an-unstoppable-wave (accessed 14 June 2019).

Masika, R (Ed.) (2002), *Gender, Development, and Climate Change*, Oxfam, Oxford.

Mathiesen, K (2018), 'EU says no new trade deals with countries not in Paris Agreement', Climate Home News, available at: http://www.climatechangenews.com/2018/02/02/eu-difficult-imagine-trade-deals-countries-not-paris-agreement/ (accessed 14 June 2019).

Matias, DM (2017), *Slow Onset Climate Change Impacts: Global Trends and the Role of Science-Policy Partnerships*, DIE (Deutsches Institut für Entwicklungspolitik), Bonn, available at: https://www.die-gdi.de/uploads/media/DP_24.2017.pdf (accessed 14 June 2019).

Mattoo, A and A Subramanian (2013), *Four Changes to Trade Rules to Facilitate Climate Change Action*, CGD Policy Paper 021, Center for Global Development, Washington, DC, available at: http://www.cgdev.org/publication/four-changes-trade (accessed 14 June 2019).

Mavroidis, PC (2007), *Trade in Goods*, Oxford University Press, Oxford.

Metz, B, OR Davidson, PR Bosch, R Dave and LA Meyer (Eds.) (2007), *Climate Change 2007: Mitigation. Contribution of Working Group III to the Fourth Assessment Report of the Intergovernmental Panel on Climate Change*, Cambridge University Press, Cambridge.

Mohammed, EY and ZB Uraguche (2013), 'Impact of climate change on fisheries: implication for the sector in sub-Saharan Africa', in Hanjra, MA (Ed.), *Global Food Security*, Nova Science Publishers, 113–35.

Monfort, CM (2015), *The Role of Women in the Seafood Industry*, Globefish Research Programme **Vol. 119**, Rome: FAO.

Montes, M (2016), 'Gender equity in export manufacturing', note for UNCTAD Expert Meeting.

Muralidharan, A, J Fehringer, S Pappa, E Rottach, M Das and M Mandal (2015), *Transforming Gender Norms, Roles, and Power Dynamics for Better Health: Evidence from a Systematic Review of Gender-Integrated Health Programs in Low- and Middle-Income Countries*, Futures Group, Health Policy Project, Washington, DC.

Neis, B, C Abord-Hugon and M Larkin (1996), Canada, in Globalization, Gender and Fisheries, Report of the Senegal Workshop on Gender Perspectives in Fisheries. Women in Fisheries Series No. 4. Samudra DOSSIER, Chennai: International Collective in Support of Fishworkers http://aquaticcommons.org/262/1/WIF_4.pdf

Nellemann, C, R Verma and L Hislop (Eds.) (2011), *Women at the Frontline of Climate Change: Gender Risks and Hope*, UNEP, Nairobi.

Neumayer, E and T Plumper (2007), 'The gendered nature of natural disasters: the impact of catastrophic events on the gender gap in life expectancy, 1981–2002', *Annals of the Association of American Geographers*, Vol. 97(3), 551–66.

Niang, I., O.C. Ruppel, M.A. Abdrabo, A. Essel, C. Lennard, J. Padgham and P. Urquhart, 2014: Africa. In: *Climate Change 2014: Impacts, Adaptation, and Vulnerability. Part B: Regional Aspects. Contribution of Working Group II to the Fifth Assessment Report of the Intergovernmental Panel on Climate Change* [Barros, V.R., C.B. Field, D.J. Dokken, M.D. Mastrandrea, K.J. Mach, T.E. Bilir, M. Chatterjee, K.L. Ebi, Y.O. Estrada, R.C. Genova, B. Girma, E.S. Kissel, A.N. Levy, S. MacCracken, P.R. Mastrandrea and L.L. White (eds.)]. Cambridge University Press, Cambridge, United Kingdom and New York, NY, USA, pp. 1199–1265.

NORAD (2016), 'Strengthening the role of women in fisheries and aquaculture', Norwegian Agency for Development Cooperation, available at: https://norad.

no/en/front/thematic-areas/climate-change-and-environment/fisheries/strengthening-the-role-of-women-in-fisheries-and-aquaculture/ (accessed 14 June 2019).

North, A (2010), 'Drought, drop out and early marriage: feeling the effects of climate change in East Africa', *Equals: Newsletter for Beyond Access* 24, http://www.e4conference.org/wp-content/uploads/2010/02/Equals24.pdf (accessed 05 September 2019).

Nurse, L.A., R.F. McLean, J. Agard, L.P. Briguglio, V. Duvat-Magnan, N. Pelesikoti, E. Tompkins and A. Webb, 2014: Small islands. In: *Climate Change 2014: Impacts, Adaptation, and Vulnerability. Part B: Regional Aspects. Contribution of Working Group II to the Fifth Assessment Report of the Intergovernmental Panel on ClimateChange* [Barros, V.R., C.B. Field, D.J. Dokken, M.D. Mastrandrea, K.J. Mach, T.E. Bilir, M. Chatterjee, K.L. Ebi, Y.O. Estrada, R.C. Genova, B. Girma, E.S. Kissel, A.N. Levy, S. MacCracken, P.R. Mastrandrea and L.L. White (eds.)]. Cambridge University Press, Cambridge, United Kingdom and New York, NY, USA, pp. 1613–1654.

Olsson, L., M. Opondo, P. Tschakert, A. Agrawal, S.H. Eriksen, S. Ma, L.N. Perch and S.A. Zakieldeen, 2014: Livelihoods and poverty. In: *Climate Change 2014: Impacts, Adaptation, and Vulnerability. Part A: Global and Sectoral Aspects. Contribution of Working Group II to the Fifth Assessment Report of the Intergovernmental Panel on Climate Change* [Field, C.B., V.R. Barros, D.J. Dokken, K.J. Mach, M.D. Mastrandrea, T.E. Bilir, M. Chatterjee, K.L. Ebi, Y.O. Estrada, R.C. Genova, B. Girma, E.S. Kissel, A.N. Levy, S. MacCracken, P.R. Mastrandrea and L.L. White (eds.)]. Cambridge University Press, Cambridge, United Kingdom and New York, NY, USA, pp. 793–832.

OECD (2012), *Green Growth and Developing Countries: A Summary for Policy Makers*, OECD, Paris.

OECD (2014a), *OECD Social Institutions and Gender Index: 2014 Synthesis Report*, available at: https://www.oecd.org/dev/development-gender/BrochureSIGI2015-web.pdf (accessed 14 June 2019).

OECD (2014b), *Green Growth and Aquaculture*, TAD/FI (2012)/Final, OECD, Paris.

OECD and IEA (2018), Update on recent progress in reform of inefficient fossil fuel subsidies that encourage wasteful consumption. https://www.oecd.org/fossil-fuels/publication/update-progress-reform-fossil-fuel-subsidies-g20.pdf (accessed 7 August 2019).

Ortiz-Barreda, G (n.d.), 'Violence against women and climate change: what does the evidence say?', paper presented at the conference Human Side of Climate Change, available at: https://www.uib.no/sites/w3.uib.no/files/attachments/ortizbarredag._cc_and_vaw.pdf (accessed 14 June 2019).

Oxfam (2005), 'The tsunami's impact on women', available at: http://www.oxfam.org.uk/what_we_do/issues/conflict_disasters/downloads/bn_tsunami_women.pdf (accessed 3 May 2005).

Paul, S (2016), 'From rape to disasters, climate change a threat to women: funders', Reuters World News, 20 May, available at https://www.reuters.com/article/us-climatechange-women-finance-idUSKCN0YB1V5 (accessed 14 June 2019).

Pearl-Martinez, R (2014), *Women at the Forefront of the Clean Energy Future*, White Paper, Initiative Gender Equality for Climate Change Opportunities (GECCO), IUCN-USAID, Washington, DC.

Pera, L and D McLaren (1999), *Globalization, Tourism & Indigenous Peoples: What You Should Know about the World's Largest 'Industry'*, Rethinking Tourism Project, St Paul, MN.

Petersen, K (1997) 'From the field: gender issues in disaster response and recovery', *Natural Hazards Observer on Women and Disasters*, **21** (5) (May 1997).

Pleumarom, A (1999), *The Hidden Costs of the New Tourisms: A Focus on Biopiracy*, Briefing Paper for CSD7 No. 1, New Frontiers, Third World Network (TWN).

Prebble, M and A Rojas (2017), *Energizing Equality: The Importance of Integrating Gender Equality Principles in National Energy Policies and Frameworks*, IUCN and USAID, Washington, DC.

Presteman, JP (2000), 'Public access and private timber harvest', *Environmental and Resource Economics*, Vol. **17**(4), 3, 11–334.

Ratna, RS (2010a) *Mainstreaming Gender through India's Foreign Trade Policy*, Centre for WTO Studies and Indian Institute of Foreign Trade, New Delhi.

Ratna, RS (2010b), 'Mainstreaming gender in trade policy & negotiations: case of India', paper presented at the ESCAP/UNDP/ARTNeT Workshop on Trade and Gender Linkages, 15–17 September, Bangkok.

Republic of Seychelles (2015), Intended Nationally Determined Contribution (INDC) Under The United Nations Framework Convention On Climate Change (UNFCCC). https://www4.unfccc.int/sites/submissions/INDC/Published%20Documents/Seychelles/1/INDC%20of%20Seychelles.pdf

Rodriguez Acha, MA (2016), 'How young feminists are tackling climate justice in 2016', *Huffington Post*. 7 March 2016. https://womendeliver.org/press/young-feminists-tackling-climate-justice-2016/ (accessed 05 September 2019).

Röhr, U (2006), 'Gender and climate change', *Tiempo* **59**, 3–7.

SADC (2016), SADC Executive Secretary, Dr. *Stergomena Lawrence-Tax on the occasion of the official opening of the meeting of SADCs ministers responsible for gender/women's affairs, 23 June* **2016**, Gaborone.

Sangho, Y, P Labaste and C Ravry (2010), *Growing Mali's Mango Exports: Linking Farmers to Markets through Innovations in the Value Chain*, World Bank, Washington, DC.

Shark, D. (2015), Keynote AddressbBy WTO Deputy Director-General David Shark. UNCTAD Informal Briefing Session, Climate Change, SDGs and Trade: At The Crossroads of Sustainable Development. 10 February 2015, Palais Des Nations, Geneva, Switzerland.

Scientific American (n.d.), 'Mosquito-borne diseases on the uptick – thanks to global warming', available at: https://www.scientificamerican.com/article/mosquito-borne-diseases-on-the-uptick-thanks-to-global-warming/ (accessed 14 June 2019).

Seguino, S (2009), 'The global economic crisis, its gender implications, and policy responses', paper prepared for Gender Perspectives on the Financial Crisis Panel at the Fifty-Third Session of the Commission on the Status of Women, United Nations, 5 March, available at: https://www.uvm.edu/~sseguino/pdf/global_crisis.pdf (accessed 14 June 2019).

Shen, W and M Power (2017), 'Africa and the export of China's clean energy revolution', *Third World Quarterly*, Vol. **38**(3), 678–97. doi: 10.1080/01436597.2016.1199262.

Simpson, MC, D Scott, M Harrison, R Sim, N Silver, E O'Kee, S Harrison, M Taylor, G Lizcano, M Rutty, H Stager, J Oldham, M Wilson, M New, J Clarke, OJ Day, N Fields, J Georges, R Waithe and P McSharry (2010), *Quantification and Magnitude of Losses and Damages Resulting from the Impacts of Climate Change: Modelling the Transformational Impacts and Costs of Sea Level Rise in the Caribbean*, United Nations Development Programme (UNDP), Bridgetown, Barbados, West Indies.

Skinner, E (2011), *Gender and Climate Change: Overview Report, BRIDGE*. Brighton: IDS, University of Sussex.

Sorensen, C, V Murray, J Lemery and J Balbus (2018), 'Climate change and women's health: impacts and policy directions', *PLoS Med*, Vol. **15**(7), e1002603. doi: 10.1371/journal.pmed.1002603.

Soroptimist International of the Americas (2008), *Reaching Out to Women when Disaster Strikes*, available at: http://www.soroptimist.org/whitepapers/WhitePaperDocs/WPReachingWomenDisaster.pdf (accessed 14 June 2019).

Sterner, T (2015), 'Economics: higher costs of climate change', *Nature*, Vol. **527**, 177–78.

Stupnytska, A, K Koch, A McBeath, S Lawson and K Matsui (2014), *Giving Credit Where It Is Due*, Goldman Sachs Global Market Institute, available at: https://www.goldmansachs.com/insights/public-policy/gmi-folder/gmi-report-pdf.pdf (accessed 14 June 2019).

Sulaiman, S (2007), 'How is climate change shifting Africa's malaria map?', SciDevnet 01/08/07, available at: https://www.scidev.net/sub-saharan-africa/malaria/opinion/how-is-climate-change-shifting-africas-malaria-ma-ssa.html (accessed 05 September 2019).

Sustainable Energy for All (2018), *Global Tracking Framework*, available at: https://www.iea.org/media/freepublications/oneoff/GlobalTrackingFramework Overview.pdf (accessed 14 June 2019).

Tahseen, J (2012), 'Global trade and climate change challenges: a brief overview of impacts on food security and gender issues', *International Journal of Climate Change Strategies and Management*, Vol. **4**(4), 442–51, available at: https://doi.org/10.1108/17568691211277755 (accessed 14 June 2019).

Tandon, N (2003), *Micro and Small Enterprise and ICT: A Gender Analysis*, unpublished paper prepared for the World Bank.

Taylor, MA, TS Stephenson, AA Chen and KA Stephenson (2012), 'Climate change and the Caribbean: review and response', *Caribbean Studies*, Vol. **40**(2), 169–200.

Tejani, S and W Milberg (2010), *Global Defeminization? Industrial Upgrading, Occupational Segmentation and Manufacturing Employment in Middle-Income Countries*, Schwartz Center for Economic Policy Analysis Working Paper, Schwartz Center for Economic Policy Analysis, New York.

Tinker, I (1994), *Urban Agriculture Is Already Here: Cities Feeding People*, IDRC, Ottawa.

Tran, C (2010), 'Using GATT, Art XX to justify climate change measures in claims under the WTO agreements', *Environmental and Planning Law Journal*, Vol. **27**(5), 346–59.

Twarog, S (1999), *Trade, Sustainable Development and Gender in the Forestry Sector*, available at: http://citeseerx.ist.psu.edu/viewdoc/download?doi=10.1.1.204.4433&rep=rep1&type=pdf (accessed 11 June 2019).

UN (2015). Addis Ababa Action Agenda of the Third International Conference on Financing for Development. New York. UN https://www.un.org/esa/ffd/wp-content/uploads/2015/08/AAAA_Outcome.pdf

UNCTAD (n.d.), 'Trade and the Sustainable Development Goals (SDGs)', available at: https://unctad.org/en/Pages/DITC/Trade-Analysis/TAB-Trade-and-SDGs.aspx (accessed 14 June 2019).

UNCTAD (1999), Trade, Sustainable Development and Gender, Papers prepared in support of the themes discussed at the Pre-UNCTAD X Expert Workshop on Trade, Sustainable Development and Gender (Geneva, 12-13 July 1999). Geneva and New York: United Nations. https://unctad.org/en/docs/poedm_m78.en.pdf (accessed 05 September 2019).

UNCTAD (2013), 'Using trade to empower women', paper presented at the UNCTAD Discussion Forum 'Why trade matters in development strategies?', 27–29 November, Palais des Nations, Geneva.

UNCTAD (2014), *Looking at Trade Policy through a 'Gender Lens': Summary of Seven Country Case Studies Conducted by UNCTAD*, Geneva: UNCTA. https://unctad.org/en/PublicationsLibrary/ditc2014d3_en.pdf (accessed 05 September 2019).

UNCTAD (2015), 'Briefing session on climate change, sustainable development goals and trade: at the crossroads of sustainable development', 10 February, Geneva, available at: https://unctad.org/en/pages/MeetingDetails.aspx?meetingid=734 (accessed 14 June 2019).

UNCTAD (2016), *Report of the Expert Meeting on Trade as a Tool for the Economic Empowerment of Women, 23 and 24 May 2016*. Geneva: UNCTAD. https://unctad.org/meetings/en/SessionalDocuments/ciem8d3_en.pdf (accessed 05 September 2019).

UNCTAD (2019), Investment Policy Hub, Geneva: UNCTAD. https://investmentpolicy.unctad.org/

UNDESA (2005), 'Enhancing participation of women in development through an enabling environment for achieving gender equality and the advancement of women: Expert Group Meeting', November 2005, available at: http://www.un.org/womenwatch/daw/egm/enabling-environment2005/index.html (accessed 14 June 2019).

UNDP (2009), *Case Study on the Impact of Climate Change on Water and Sanitation in Jamaica*, (prepared for UNDP by Linnette Vassell), UNDP, Barbados.

UNDP (2009), *Case Study on the Impact of Climate Change on Agriculture on an Indigenous Community in Guyana*, prepared for the UNDP by Paulette Bynoe. UNDP Barbados

UNDP (2011), *Ensuring Gender Equity in Climate Change Financing*, UNDP/GGCA, New York.

UNDP (2015), *Energy Efficiency NAMA in the Garment Industry in Cambodia*, available at: http://www.undp.org/content/undp/en/home/librarypage/environment-energy/mdg-carbon/NAMAs/energy-efficiency-nama-in-the-garment-industry-in-cambodia.html (accessed 14 June 2019).

Bibliography

UNDP (2016) African Human Development Report, UNDP New York. Available at https://www.undp.org/content/undp/en/home/librarypage/hdr/2016-africa-human-development-report.html (accessed 9 August 2019).

UNDP and GGCA (2009), *Resource Guide on Gender and Climate Change*. UNDP and GGCA.

UNECA (2010), *Gender and Climate Change: Women Matter*, working paper, October.

UN Economic and Social Council (ECOSOC), *UN Economic and Social Council Resolution 1997/2: Agreed Conclusions,* 18 July 1997, 1997/2, available at: https://www.refworld.org/docid/4652c9fc2.html [accessed 14 September 2019]

UN Economic Commission for Latin America and the Caribbean (UNECLAC) (2005), *Grenada: A Gender Impact Assessment of Hurricane Ivan – Making the Invisible Visible*. Santiago: UN ECLAC

UNFCCC (n.d.) Nationally Appropriate Mitigation Actions (NAMAs). https://unfccc.int/topics/mitigation/workstreams/nationally-appropriate-mitigation-actions

UNFCCC (n.d.a), 'Economic diversification', available at: http://unfccc.int/adaptation/workstreams/nairobi_work_programme/items/3994.php (accessed 14 June 2019).

UNFCCC (n.d.b), Decision 18.CP/20 (2014 – COP20), Lima Work Programme on Gender, available at: https://unfccc.int/sites/default/files/auv_cop20_gender.pdf (accessed 05 September 2019

UNFCCC (n.d.c), 'Climate-related risks and extreme events', available at: https://unfccc.int/topics/resilience/resources/climate-related-risks-and-extreme-events (accessed 05 September 2019) https://unfccc.int/topics/resilience/resources/climate-related-risks-and-extreme-events (accessed 14 June 2019).

UNFCCC (2013), *Report on Gender Composition: Note by the Secretariat*, United Nations Framework Convention, Bonn.

UNFCCC (2014), *Report on the Meeting on Available Tools for the Use of Indigenous and Traditional Knowledge and Practices for Adaptation, Needs of Local and Indigenous Communities and the Application of Gender-Sensitive Approaches and Tools for Adaptation*, FCCC/SBST A/2014/INF.11.

UNFCCC (2015), *Report on the In-Session Workshop on Gender-Responsive Climate Policy with a Focus on Mitigation Action and Technology Development and Transfer: Note by the Secretariat*, Item 14 of the provisional agenda Gender and Climate Change, Subsidiary Body for Implementation Forty-third session, Paris, 30 November to 11 December.

UNFCCC Secretariat (2015), *Draft Compilation of Decisions, Subsidiary Body Reports and Adopted Conclusions Related to Gender and Climate Change*, GCC/DRC/2015/1, 21 May, UNFCCC Secretariat.

UNIFEM (2009), *Findings of the Baseline Studies on Women in Informal Cross Border Trade in Africa*, Brussels.

UNIFEM (2010), *Unleashing the Potential of Women Informal Cross Border Traders to Transform Intra-African Trade*, UNIFEM, New York.

UNISDR (2013), *Issues of Vulnerability with Specific Reference to Gender in the Asia-Pacific: Post-2015 Framework for Disaster Risk Reduction Consultations*, background paper.

United Nations (n.d.), 'Action on climate and SDGs', available at: https://cop23.unfccc.int/achieving-the-sustainable-development-goals-through-climate-action (accessed on 12 June 2019).

UN REDD (2013) Guidance Note on Gender Sensitive REDD+ https://www.undp.org/content/dam/undp/library/gender/Gender%20and%20Environment/Guidance%20Note%20Gender%20Sensitive%20REDD%20English_FINAL.pdf (accessed 05 September 2019).

UN-REDD (2009), available at www.un-redd.org.

UN Women (n.d.), *Women, Gender Equality and Climate Change*, fact sheet.

UN Women (2014), World Survey on the Role of Women in Development 2014: Gender Equality and Sustainable Development. New York: UN Women

UN Women (2016), Leveraging co-benefits between gender equality and climate action for sustainable development. Mainstreaming gender considerations in climate change projects. New York: UN Women.

UN Women (2016), 'Empowering women through climate-smart agriculture in the DRC', available at: https://africa.unwomen.org/en/news-and-events/stories/2016/11/empowering-women-through-climate-smart-agriculture-in-the-drc (accessed 05 September 2019). http://africa.unwomen.org/en/news-and-events/stories/2016/11/empowering-women-through-climate-smart-agriculture-in-the-drc (accessed 14 June 2019).

UN Women (2017), *Brief on Economic Empowerment of Women*, UN Women, New York.

UN Women (2018), *Turning Promises into Action: Gender Equality in the 2030 Agenda for Sustainable Development*, United Nations, UN Women, New York.

UN World Commission on Environment and Development (1987) 'Our Common Future.' The Brundtland Report. https://sustainabledevelopment.un.org/content/documents/5987our-common-future.pdf (Accessed 29 July 2019).

UN WTO (2011), *Harnessing trade for sustainable development and a green economy*. https://www.wto.org/english/res_e/publications_e/brochure_rio_20_e.pdf (Accessed 2 August 2019).

UNWTO (2015), *Tourism and the Sustainable Development Goals*. World Tourism Organization. Madrid, Spain: UNWTO http://cf.cdn.unwto.org/sites/all/files/pdf/sustainable_development_goals_brochure.pdf (accessed 05 September 2019).

UNWTO and the Global Compact Network Spain (2017), *The Tourism Sector and the Sustainable Development Goals: Responsible Tourism, a Global Commitment*, UNWTO and United Nations Global Compact Network Spain. Madrid: UNWTO. http://cf.cdn.unwto.org/sites/all/files/pdf/turismo_responsable_omt_acc.pdf (accessed 05 September 2019).

UNWTO and UNDP (2017), *Tourism and the Sustainable Development Goals: Journey to 2030*. Madrid: UNWTO. https://www.undp.org/content/dam/undp/library/Sustainable%20Development/UNWTO_UNDP_Tourism%20and%20the%20SDGs.pdf (accessed 05 September 2019).

USAID (2009), *Promoting Gender Equitable Opportunities: Why It Matters for Agricultural Value Chains*, US Agency for International Development, Washington, DC.

USAID and COMFISH (2012), *Annual Report October 2011 – September 2012 USAID/ COMFISH Project PENCOO GEJ Collaborative Management for a Sustainable Fisheries Future in Senegal*, USAID, Senegal.

van Aelst, K and N Holvoet (2016), 'Intersections of marital status in accessing climate change adaptation: evidence from rural Tanzania', *World Development*, Vol. **79**, 40–50.

van Staveren, I, D Elson, C Grown and N Cagatay (2007), *The Feminist Economics of Trade*, London: Routledge.

Wallach, L and M Sforza (1999), *The WTO: Five Years of Reasons to Resist Corporate Globalization*, New York: Seven Stories Press.

Walsh, C (2015), 'Life, nature and gender otherwise: feminist reflections and provocations from the Andes', in Harcourt, W and IL Nelson (Eds.), *Practising Feminist Political Ecologies Moving Beyond the 'Green Economy'*, Zed Books.

Waskey, AJ (2007), 'Nontraditional agricultural exports (NTAEs)', in Robbins, P (Ed.), *Encyclopedia of Environment and Society*, SAGE Knowledge. available at: http://sk.sagepub.com/reference/environment/n778.xml (accessed 14 June 2019).

Water Justice Project (n.d.), Amsterdam: the The Transnational Institute (TNI) http://blueplanetproject.net/

Wedderburn, J and J Grant Cummings (2017), *A Concept Paper: A Review and Gender Analysis of the 'Climate Change Policy Framework for Jamaica' Submitted to the Climate Change Division, Ministry of Economic Growth and Job Creation*, 13 October 2017.

WEDO (2012), *Women's Participation in the UNFCCC 2008–2012*, Women's Environment and Development Organization, New York.

WEDO (2016), *A Gender Analysis of Intended Nationally Determined Contributions (2016)*, available at: http://wedo.org/%EF%BF%BC%EF%BF%BCresearch-paper-gender-analysis-indcs/ (accessed 14 June 2019).

Westberg, J (2010), 'The WTO permissibility of border trade measures in climate change mitigation', master's thesis, Lund University, available at: http://www.tradeandenvironmentnexus.com/wp-content/uploads/2011/12/The-WTO-permissibility-of-border-trade-measures-in-climate-change-mitigation.pdf (accessed 14 June 2019).

WHO 2010a Gender inequities in environment and health Chap 10, p. 217–238 in Environment and health risks: a review of the influence and effects of social inequalities. Copenhagen: WHO Regional Office for Europe.

WHO (2010b), *Gender, Climate Change and Health*, available at: http://www.who.int/globalchange/GenderClimateChangeHealthfinal.pdf (accessed 14 June 2019).

WHO (2014), *Climate Change and Health: A Tool to Estimate Health and Adaptation Costs*, WHO Regional Office for Europe, Copenhagen.

Williams, M (2002), *The Political Economy of Tourism Liberalization, Gender and the GATS*, International Gender and Trade Secretariat, Center of Concern, Washington, DC.

Williams, M (2003), *Gender Issues in the Multilateral Trading System*, Commonwealth Secretariat, London.

Williams, M (2013), *Integrating a Gender Perspective in Climate Change, Development Policy and the UNFCCC*. Geneva: South Centre.

Williams, M (2015), *Gender and Climate Financing: Coming Out of the Margin*, Routledge, London.

Williams, M (2016), UNCTAD's Work on Gender and Trade: Progress and Challenges. Prepared for UNCTAD XIV. Geneva: South Centre.

Williams, M (2017), *The Caribbean and Climate Change: Challenges for Development and Social and Gender Equity*, Friedrich Ebert Stiftung, Regions Refocus and South Centre. Bonn: FES.

Williams, M (2018), *Using Trade to Empower Women: Pitfalls and Progression*, South Centre, Geneva.

Williams, M (2019a), *Gender Trade and Climate: An Overview*, policy brief, South Centre, Geneva.

Williams, M (2019b), *Gender in the Middle: The Trade and Climate and Women's Empowerment Dynamics*, Gender and Trade Coalition. Geneva: South Centre.

Women's Environmental Network (2010), *The Impacts of Climate Change on Women and Public Policy*, available at: https://www.gdnonline.org/resources/Gender%20and%20the%20climate%20change%20agenda%2021.pdf (accessed 14 June 2019).

World Bank (2009), 'Gender in fisheries and aquaculture', in Voegele, J., M. Villarreal and R. Cooke (Eds.), *Gender in Agriculture Source Book: Module 13*, 561–600. Washington, D.C.: World Bank.

World Bank (2011), *Gender and Climate: Things You Should Know*, World Bank, Washington, DC.

World Bank (2012), *Agricultural Innovation Systems – An Investment Source Book*. Agriculture and Rural Development, Geneva: World Bank, available at: http://siteresources.worldbank.org/INTARD/Resources/335807-1330620492317/9780821386842.pdf (accessed 05 September 2019). http://go.worldbank.org/YR16K0VVB0 (accessed 14 June 2019).

World Bank (2012c), *Hidden Harvest: The Global Contribution of Captured Fisheries*, World Bank, FAO and WorldFish Center. Washington, D.C.: World Bank

World Bank Group and World Trade Organization, 2015. *The Role of Trade in Ending Poverty*. World Trade Organization: Geneva.

World Bank (2015b) Gender Data Portal. Washington, D.C.: World Bank.

World Bank (2016a), *Women, Business and the Law*, World Bank, Washington, DC.

World Bank (2016b), Doing Business. Washington, D.C.: World Bank.

World Bank (2017), *Doing Business*. Washington, D.C.: World Bank.

World Bank (2018), *Global Economic Prospects, January 2018*, World Bank, Washington, DC.

World Bank (2019a), 'Africa Program for Fisheries', available at: www.worldbank.org/en/programs/africa-program-for-fisheries (accessed 14 June 2019).

World Bank (2019b), SE4ALL Data base for SE4ALL Global Tracking Framework, available at: https://www.worldbank.org/en/topic/energy/publication/Global-Tracking-Framework-Report (accessed 05 September 2019). https://data.worldbank.org/indicator/eg.elc.accs.zs (accessed 9 April 2019).

World Bank, FAO and IFAD (2009), *Gender in Agriculture: Source Book*, Agriculture and Rural Development Series, World Bank E-library, World Bank, Geneva.

World Bank, FAO and WorldFish Centre (2010), *The Hidden Harvests: The Global Contribution of Capture Fisheries*, World Bank, Washington, DC.

World Conference on Disaster Reduction (2015), *High Level Multi-Stakeholder Partnership Dialogue 'Mobilizing Women's Leadership for Disaster Risk Reduction' – Summary Report for Plenary Meeting on 18 March*, available at: http://www.wcdrr.org/uploads/Dialogue-1-co-Chairs-Summary1.pdf (accessed 14 June 2019).

WorldFish Center (2019) News Updates. Bangladesh: World Fish Center. https://www.worldfishcenter.org/news-updates

WTO (n.d.), 'Climate change and the potential relevance of WTO rules', available at: https://www.wto.org/english/tratop_e/envir_e/climate_measures_e.htm (accessed 12 June 2019).

WTO (nd2), WTO website. Understanding the WTO: Basics Principles of the trading system. https://www.wto.org/english/thewto_e/whatis_e/tif_e/fact2_e.htm (accessed 05 September 2019).

WTO (2011) DOHA WTO Ministerial Declaration. WT/MIN(01)DEC/1 https://www.wto.org/english/thewto_e/minist_e/min01_e/mindecl_e.htm (accessed 2 August 2019).

WTO (2012), 'An introduction to trade and environment in the WTO', available online at: https://www.wto.org/english/tratop_e/envir_e/envt_intro_e.htm (accessed 13 December 2012).

WTO (2013), 'Lamy calls for dialogue on trade and energy in the WTO', available online at: https://www.wto.org/english/news_e/sppl_e/sppl279_e.htm (accessed 7 August 2018).

WTO (2017a), *Gender Aware Trade Policy: A Springboard for Women's Economic Empowerment*, WTO, Geneva.

WTO (2017b), 'Buenos Aires Declaration on Women and Trade outlines actions to empower women', available at: https://www.wto.org/english/news_e/news17_e/mc11_12dec17_e.htm (accessed 14 June 2019).

WTO (2017c), *Aid for Trade at a Glance 2017*, WTO and OECD, Geneva.

WTO (2017d), 'Buenos Aires ministerial statement on Fossil Fuel subsidies reform,' available at: https://www.wto.org/english/thewto_e/minist_e/mc11_e/documents_e.htm (accessed 7 August 2019).

WTO (2019) Activities of the WTO and the challenge of climate change https://www.wto.org/english/tratop_e/envir_e/climate_challenge_e.htm (Accessed 5 September 2019).

WTO and UNEP (2009), *Trade and Climate Change: A Report by the United Nations Environment and the WTO*. Geneva: WTO and UNEP.

Yoder, A (1998), *Sustainable Development, Ecotourism, and Globalisation: Are They Compatible?* unpublished paper, University of California, Irvine.

Yoder, D (1999), 'A contingency framework for environmental decision-making: linking decisions, problems and processes', *Policy Studies Review*, Vol. **16**(3/4), 11–35.

Yuan, H, P Zhou and D Zhou (2011), 'What is low-carbon development? A conceptual analysis', *Energy Procedia*, Vol. **5**, 1706–17.

Zarilli, S (2017), 'The gender chapters in trade agreements: A true revolution?', ICTSD, Geneva, available at: http://www.ictsd.org/opinion/the-gender-chapters-in-trade-agreements-a-true-revolution (Accessed 05 September 2019).